# JOURNEY OF INFINITE DISCOVERIES

# Journey Of Infinite Discoveries

## Mack Rafeal

Noble Publishing

# *Contents*

| | |
|---|---:|
| INDEX | 1 |
| Introduction | 3 |
| Chapter 1 | 7 |
| Chapter 2 | 23 |
| Chapter 3 | 40 |
| Chapter 4 | 56 |
| Chapter 5 | 73 |
| Chapter 6 | 89 |
| Chapter 7 | 105 |
| Chapter 8 | 121 |
| Chapter 9 | 136 |

# INDEX

**Introduction**

**Chapter 1: The Call to Adventure**
1.1 Introduction to the protagonist and their ordinary world.
1.2 Something disrupts the status quo, a mysterious call to adventure.
1.3 The protagonist hesitates but ultimately decides to embark on the journey.

**Chapter 2: Crossing the Threshold**
2.1 The protagonist leaves their comfort zone and enters a new, unfamiliar world.
2.2 Encounter with mentors or guides who provide insight and tools for the journey.
2.3 Initial challenges and doubts emerge, testing the protagonist's resolve.

**Chapter 3: Trials and Tribulations**
3.1 Series of challenges and obstacles that the protagonist must overcome.
3.2 Developments in character, skills, and knowledge.
3.3 Introduction to allies and adversaries who play crucial roles.

**Chapter 4: The Abyss**
4.1 The protagonist faces a major setback or crisis.
4.2 A moment of profound self-discovery and transformation.
4.3 Internal and external conflicts reach a climax.

**Chapter 5: Revelation and Insight**
5.1 The protagonist gains a deeper understanding of themselves and the purpose of the journey.

5.2 Unveiling of hidden truths and mysteries.

5.3 Integration of newfound wisdom to navigate the path ahead.

**Chapter 6: The Road Less Traveled**

6.1 The journey takes unexpected turns, leading to unexplored territories.

6.2 Exploration of diverse landscapes, cultures, and perspectives.

6.3 The protagonist confronts personal biases and broadens their worldview.

**Chapter 7: Resurrection and Redemption**

7.1 The protagonist faces the ultimate challenge or adversary.

7.2 Application of lessons learned and growth achieved throughout the journey.

7.3 Redemption and emergence as a transformed individual.

**Chapter 8: The Return**

8.1 The protagonist contemplates the insights gained and the impact of the journey.

8.2 Reintegration into the ordinary world, bringing newfound wisdom.

8.3 Reflection on personal growth and the significance of the discoveries.

**Chapter 9: The Ever-Unfolding Journey**

9.1 The conclusion reflects on the ongoing nature of discovery.

9.2 The protagonist realizes that the journey never truly ends.

9.3 Open-ended possibilities for future adventures and explorations.

# Introduction

In the huge embroidery of human life, the excursion of boundless disclosures unfurls as a complex investigation of the obscure, a never-ending journey for understanding, and a steady quest for information. From the earliest snapshots of cognizance, people have been driven by an intrinsic interest that rises above the limits of existence. This excursion is a demonstration of the dauntless human soul, perpetually pushed by the craving to disentangle the secrets of the universe, both inside and then some.

At the core of this odyssey lies the voracious hunger for disclosure, a natural power that has impelled mankind from the crude caverns to the levels of mechanical wonders. An excursion traverses centuries, including the ages of old civic establishments, the upheavals of logical request, and the groundbreaking jumps of the computerized age. The quest for information has been the directing star, controlling developments through the flows of history, molding societies, and manufacturing the actual texture of human character.

The excursion of endless disclosures is profoundly imbued in the human mind, woven into the texture of our shared perspective. From the early agrarian social orders to the high level developments of today, the drive to investigate, comprehend, and improve has been a steady friend. It is an excursion set apart by the two victories and hardships, by snapshots of edification and times of lack of definition, yet continuously pushing ahead in a tireless walk towards the wildernesses of the unexplored world.

As the human species developed, so did the techniques for investigation and revelation. The people of yore explored strange domains, both geological and scholarly, directed by the stars and moved by the breezes of interest. The extraordinary civic establishments of Mesopotamia, Egypt, Greece, and Rome made a permanent imprint on the guide of human advancement, each adding to the supply of information that would be acquired by people in the future.

With the beginning of the Renaissance, the excursion of limitless disclosures arrived at an essential second. The recovery of traditional learning, the development of the print machine, and the soul of request introduced a time of uncommon scholarly age. Visionaries like Leonardo da Vinci, Galileo Galilei, and Johannes Kepler prepared for another comprehension of the universe, testing the dug in convictions of their time and establishing the groundworks for the logical transformation.

The Edification, a scholarly development that moved throughout Europe in the seventeenth and eighteenth hundreds of years, further powered the blazes of revelation. Masterminds like Voltaire, Rousseau, and Locke supported reason, individual freedoms, and the logical technique. The quest for information turned into an ethical goal, and the logical technique arose as a useful asset for opening the privileged insights of the normal world.

The nineteenth century saw a blast of revelations across different fields, driven by headways in innovation and a developing modern culture. Charles Darwin's hypothesis of development reshaped how we might interpret life's beginnings, while the intermittent table, a demonstration of Dmitri Mendeleev's virtuoso, coordinated the components into an intelligent structure. The message and later the phone reformed correspondence, contracting the world and associating far off corners of the globe.

The twentieth century denoted an age of unrivaled advancement and disturbance. From the speculations of relativity and quantum mechanics that re-imagined how we might interpret the universe to the creation of the PC that changed the actual structure holding the system together, the speed of disclosure sped up dramatically. The logical and innovative accomplishments of this time, including space investigation, hereditary designing, and the web, impelled mankind into unknown regions of information and capacity.

In the domain of medication, leap forwards, for example, the disclosure of antitoxins and immunizations changed medical care, expanding human life expectancy and relieving the effect of once-lethal sicknesses. The disentangling of the human genome opened new outskirts in hereditary qualities, offering extraordinary experiences into the complexities of life itself. These progressions, brought into the world of vigorous examination and advancement, highlighted the extraordinary force of the excursion of limitless revelations in working on the human condition.

All the while, artistic expression and humanities encountered their very own renaissance. Writing, music, and the visual expressions went through significant changes, mirroring the turbulent social and social changes of the time. From the cutting edge developments that provoked conventional standards to the worldwide impacts molding a multicultural world, the excursion of endless revelations reached out past the domain of science and innovation, incorporating the rich embroidery of human articulation and inventiveness.

As mankind plunged into the 21st 100 years, the scene of revelation kept on developing, formed by the exchange of worldwide interconnectedness and remarkable innovative progressions. The computerized age achieved a democratization of data, cultivating another period of cooperation and network. The web, a result of human resourcefulness, turned into an immense store of information, a stage for talk, and an impetus for development on a worldwide scale.

The excursion of boundless revelations, in any case, isn't without its difficulties and moral contemplations. The very innovations that have achieved momentous leap forwards additionally present situations about protection, security, and the moral ramifications of logical progressions. The interconnectedness of the cutting edge world has led to complex issues, from environmental change to worldwide wellbeing emergencies, requesting an aggregate and interdisciplinary way to deal with tracking down arrangements.

Besides, the excursion of limitless disclosures is a common human undertaking, rising above lines, societies, and belief systems. Joint effort and trade of thoughts have become fundamental to the advancement of information, cultivating a worldwide local area of scholars and trend-setters. As we explore the unknown domains of the 21st hundred years, the difficulties we face require an aggregate and comprehensive methodology, one that draws upon the insight of different points of view and encounters.

In the unfurling story of the excursion of limitless revelations, training arises as a foundation. Engaging people with the apparatuses to think basically, tackle issues, and adjust to a consistently influencing world is fundamental for the proceeded with progress of humankind. Instruction grants information as well as develops a feeling of request, empowering people to set out on their own excursions of revelation and add to the aggregate quest for understanding.

The excursion of limitless revelations is a demonstration of the versatility of the human soul and the vast capability of human insight. From the antiquated recorders scratching information onto earth tablets to the cutting edge researchers examining the secrets of the universe, every age has added its part to the continuous adventure of investigation and advancement. The excursion isn't straight yet a mosaic of interconnected ways, an impression of the different and dynamic nature of human request.

As we stand on the limit of a questionable future, the excursion of endless revelations coaxes us to wander into the obscure with boldness and interest. It moves us to stand up to the intricacies of our reality, to wrestle with the moral ramifications of our disclosures, and to produce a way toward an additional maintainable and comprehensive future. The story of this excursion is as yet being composed, formed by the decisions, the difficulties we survive, and the revelations that anticipate in the huge span of human potential.

Taking everything into account, the excursion of boundless revelations is a persevering and dynamic campaign that rises above the limits of reality. It is an adventure woven into the actual texture of human life, driven by an unquenchable interest and a tenacious quest for information. From the beginning of civilization to the intricacies of the cutting edge period, this excursion has formed the course of mankind's set of experiences, making a permanent imprint on the embroidery of human advancement. As we explore the unfamiliar regions representing things to come, the excursion of endless disclosures provokes us to embrace the obscure, to address, to investigate, and to contribute our exceptional voices to the continuous account of human investigation and understanding.

# Chapter 1

**The Call to Adventure**

The call to experience reverberations through the chronicles of mankind's set of experiences, resounding as a strong and enduring power that entices people to leave on extraordinary excursions of self-revelation, investigation, and development. This immortal and prototype call is woven into the actual texture of human life, moving incalculable legends and champions to leave the solace of the known and adventure into the unfamiliar domains of the unexplored world.

At its center, the call to experience is a challenge to break liberated from the recognizable and stand up to the secrets that lie past the limit of routine presence. It appears in horde structures — a murmur in the breeze, a longing profound inside the spirit, or an emotional disturbance that upsets the harmony of regular day to day existence. Whether unobtrusive or unmistakable, the call coaxes people to step outside the limits of the customary and set out on a journey that guarantees development, challenges, and the potential for significant change.

The charm of the call to experience is profoundly implanted in the human mind, as proven by the endless fantasies, legends, and social stories that praise the legend's excursion. From the legendary stories of Gilgamesh and Odysseus to the cutting edge realistic experiences of Luke Skywalker and Katniss Everdeen, the call to experience fills in as a general theme that rises above time and social limits. It addresses the intrinsic human craving for investigation, success, and the quest for a higher reason.

The excursion ignited by the call to experience isn't simply an actual campaign yet a significant odyssey of the spirit. It requests that people face their apprehensions, embrace vulnerability, and explore the confounded scenes of their own mind. The legend's excursion, as explained by Joseph Campbell, frames a story structure that reflects the phases of the call to experience, taking heroes from the well explored parts of the planet into the domains of the new, where they experience preliminaries, guides, and eventually, a groundbreaking apotheosis.

In the call to experience, there is an understood affirmation of the pressure among security and the unexplored world. It rocks the boat, welcoming people to scrutinize the schedules and designs that characterize their lives. This pressure is clear in the legendary accounts of divine beings and humans, where divinities challenge the limits of their heavenly domains to slide into the human domain, or humans rise to challenge the divine beings. A strain impels the story forward, pushing people past their usual ranges of familiarity and into the pot of self-disclosure.

The call to experience frequently shows up unbidden, getting people unsuspecting appearing unexpectedly. It can rise out of an individual emergency, a fortunate experience, or an inward yearning that won't be overlooked. At times, it appears as a tutor or an envoy, an insightful figure who bestows the call and gives direction to the legend as they set out on their excursion. Whether proclaimed by a guide or emerging from the profundities of one's own cognizance, the call to experience fills in as an impetus for change.

One of the main qualities of the call to experience is its innate uncertainty. It isn't generally clear what the excursion involves, what difficulties will be confronted, or what the final location might be. This vagueness expects people to call mental fortitude and confidence in the unfurling system of revelation. The legend's process is a demonstration of the human ability to explore vulnerability, defy misfortune, and arise changed on the opposite side.

The call to experience stretches out past the domain of fantasy and fiction; a power shapes the directions of genuine lives. Think about the business person who, driven by a dream or a thought, brings the jump into the obscure, flirting with disappointment in quest for development. Consider the craftsman who notices the call to make, digging into the openings of creative mind to deliver work that challenges shows and grows the limits of imaginative articulation. These genuine models mirror the general idea of the call to experience and its ability to push people toward unprecedented accomplishments.

On occasion, the call to experience appears as an aggregate summons, welcoming whole social orders or networks to set out on a common journey for progress and change. Unrests, social developments, and social moves frequently epitomize the aggregate reaction to a call that challenges the laid out request and coaxes towards a new and strange future. The journey for social equality, the battle against abuse, and the quest for equity are instances of aggregate calls to experience that have molded the course of history.

The call to experience isn't without its hardships. The legend's process is full of difficulties, obstructions, and snapshots of gloom. These preliminaries act as pots, testing the backbone of people and pushing them to find qualities and capacities they might not have acknowledged they had. The call requests versatility, constancy, and a readiness to defy the shadow parts of oneself.

As people answer the call to experience, they frequently experience coaches or partners who give direction, intelligence, and backing. These coaches assume a significant part in the legend's excursion, offering experiences, devices, and support to explore the difficulties ahead. The coach paradigm, whether exemplified by a savvy senior, a magical figure, or a confided in companion, addresses the aggregate insight of humankind went down through ages.

The call to experience likewise includes a course of self-revelation, where people encounter their own limits, fears, and yearnings. It is an excursion internal, a plummet into the profundities of the mind, where the legend should face their own evil spirits and go through a course of change. This internal mission is just about as fundamental as the outer difficulties looked on the excursion, for it is through self-revelation that people track down the solidarity to defeat snags and advance into their most genuine selves.

In the fabulous embroidery of mankind's set of experiences, the call to experience has been a main thrust behind investigation and revelation. From the intense pilots who set forth across strange seas to the bold voyagers who wandered into the core of neglected mainlands, the call to experience has prodded humankind to grow the limits of information and stretch the boundaries of what is conceivable. A call reverberates in the logical interest that drives scientists to test the secrets of the universe and in the mechanical development that changes the manner in which we live.

The call to experience isn't restricted to the domains of investigation and valor; it saturates the circles of reasoning, otherworldliness, and the quest for importance. Masterminds and searchers since forever ago have answered the call to leave on scholarly and profound missions, testing the predominant convictions of their time and looking for a more profound comprehension of presence. The call coaxes not exclusively to actual investigation yet additionally to the investigation of thoughts, values, and the actual idea of the real world.

As people notice the call to experience, they add to the aggregate story of human advancement. The stories of legends and champions, both legendary and verifiable, entwine to shape a rich embroidery of human experience. Every individual excursion adds a one of a kind string to this embroidery, enhancing the aggregate story of the human mission for significance, reason, and development.

In contemporary society, the call to experience keeps on repeating, welcoming people to set out on excursions of individual and aggregate importance. The computerized age has extended the skylines of investigation, offering new boondocks in virtual scenes and advanced domains. The call to improve, upset, and make has led to another type of explorers, from business people and designers to specialists and visionaries, who explore the intricacies of a quickly impacting world.

The call to experience is certainly not a one-time event however a common subject all through the human life expectancy. As people explore the various phases of life, they might experience numerous calls, each alluring them towards additional opportunities and potential open doors for development. The emotional meltdown, frequently portrayed by a reassessment of one's life and needs, is a sign of the call to experience that welcomes people to set out on a mission for validness and satisfaction.

All in all, the call to experience is a central and getting through part of the human experience. A widespread power rises above social, transient, and geological limits, molding the stories of people and social orders the same. Whether in the domains of legend, history, or regular daily existence, the call coaxes people to wander past the known, stand up to difficulties, and find the undiscovered supplies of their true capacity. The legend's excursion, with its preliminaries, guides, and changes, reflects the significant odyssey of the human soul as it answers the everlasting call to experience.

**1.1 Introduction to the protagonist and their ordinary world.**

In the tremendous domain of narrating, the prologue to the hero and their standard world fills in as the significant establishment whereupon stories unfurl. This underlying composition lays the foundation for the person's excursion, giving experiences into their life, desires, and the apparently ordinary conditions that go before the looming experience. It is inside the customary world that the hero's substance is uncovered, making way for the extraordinary odyssey that lies ahead.

At the start, the normal world addresses business as usual, a natural scene where the hero dwells before the call to experience disturbs their daily schedule. This regular climate fills a double need: it lays out a pattern for the crowd to grasp the hero's predictability, and it emphasizes the ensuing takeoff from this commonality when the excursion starts. The common world is a material whereupon the subtleties of the person's character, connections, and day to day battles are painted.

Essentially, the hero's standard world isn't just a background yet a vital part of their personality. It is here that the crowd acquires experiences into the person's qualities, inspirations, and the contentions that characterize their reality. Whether a clamoring metropolitan setting, a curious town, or a cutting edge oppressed world, the customary world exemplifies the hero's existence, offering a depiction of their life before the impelling occurrence pushes them into the unexplored world.

In the domain of exemplary writing, think about Jane Austen's "Pride and Bias." The conventional universe of Elizabeth Bennet unfurls in the respectable field of Hertfordshire, where cultural standards, familial assumptions, and the quest for adoration shape her ordinary presence. Austen carefully depicts the normal world to give perusers a far reaching comprehension of Elizabeth's cultural limitations, her familial elements, and the scene where her own process unfurls.

Additionally, in J.K. Rowling's "Harry Potter and the Alchemist's Stone," the normal world for youthful Harry is the smothering and unremarkable existence with the Dursleys at Number 4 Privet Drive. Rowling acquaints perusers with the normal world from the perspective of the abused vagrant, accentuating his disconnection, the abuse he perseveres, and the glaring difference between the common and the mysterious world that looks for him.

In true to life narrating, the common world is frequently outwardly portrayed, offering crowds an instinctive feeling of the hero's environmental elements. Take, for example, the customary universe of Luke Skywalker in George Lucas' "Star Wars: Episode IV - Another Expectation." Luke's common life on the desert planet of Tatooine, chipping away at his uncle's dampness ranch, lays out the background for his excursion. The fruitless scenes, the paired nightfall, and the unremarkable schedules of Luke's life make an unmistakable difference with the cosmic experience that looks for him.

The standard world fills a story need past simple composition. It works with crowd commitment by laying out an engaging perspective. Watchers or perusers see themselves in the standard parts of the hero's life, manufacturing an association that makes the resulting venture seriously convincing. Whether it's the preliminaries of regular connections, proficient difficulties, or individual yearnings, the standard world mirrors general human encounters.

In contemporary narrating, the common world reaches out past actual scenes to envelop the advanced domain. In a world progressively associated by innovation, heroes might explore the intricacies of virtual spaces, online connections, and the computerized scenes that shape present day presence. This development mirrors the changing elements of normal universes because of the innovative and social movements of the 21st hundred years.

Think about the normal universe of Imprint Zuckerberg in Aaron Sorkin's "The Informal organization." The film depicts Zuckerberg's excursion from a Harvard understudy exploring social elements to the formation of Facebook, in a general sense modifying the scene of human association. The standard world, for this situation, envelops both physical and computerized spaces, featuring the extraordinary effect of mechanical advancement on the customary existences of people.

As narrating advances, so does the investigation of the normal world in speculative fiction. Works of sci-fi and dream frequently push the limits of the conventional, acquainting heroes with universes where sorcery, trend setting innovation, or substitute real factors reclassify what is viewed as typical. In Philip Pullman's "The Brilliant Compass," the standard universe of youthful Lyra Belacqua traverses an equal universe where each human has a dæmon, a sign of their spirit. Pullman makes an unprecedented standard world that provokes interest and makes way for an excursion that rises above the limits of regular reality.

The conventional world is a unique story component that goes through change over the long haul. As the hero wrestles with difficulties, faces clashes, and develops as a person, the customary world turns into a liquid element. The actual idea of business as usual is reshaped by the hero's excursion, and what once appeared to be normal becomes pervaded with newly discovered importance.

This groundbreaking perspective is clear in many stories about growing up, where the common universe of immaturity is set apart by the preliminaries of self-revelation, personality development, and the quest for freedom. J.D. Salinger's

"The Catcher in the Rye" explores the customary universe of Holden Caulfield, a disappointed young person wrestling with the fakery of grown-up society. Salinger catches the pith of Holden's common world, loaded up with estrangement and a mission for realness, making way for his existential excursion.

The conventional world isn't exclusively a develop of fiction; an idea resounds, in actuality, stories. Each person, purposely or unwittingly, encounters their own standard world — a domain characterized by schedule, connections, and individual goals. It is inside this circle that life's process unfurls, and the call to experience, in its different structures, welcomes people to step past the known and into the strange regions of development and self-disclosure.

In self-portraying works, the conventional world is the material whereupon people paint the embroidered artwork of their encounters. Maya Angelou's "I Know Why the Confined Bird Sings" dives into the normal universe of her initial years, exploring the intricacies of bigotry, injury, and self-character. Angelou's story ability changes the apparently commonplace parts of her standard world into a powerful investigation of flexibility and win.

The hero's common world isn't restricted to physical or outer aspects; it includes the inner scene of feelings, convictions, and individual battles. In Hermann Hesse's "Siddhartha," the standard world for the protagonist is the profound and philosophical scene of old India. Siddhartha's process unfurls inside the domains of his own awareness as he wrestles with existential inquiries, looking for illumination and rising above the standard meanings of self.

Besides, the conventional world frequently fills in as a foil to the phenomenal difficulties and undertakings that lie ahead. The juxtaposition between the everyday and the uncommon highlights the meaning of the hero's excursion. This division is a story gadget that elevates strain, catches consideration, and stresses the groundbreaking idea of the impending mission.

With regards to mythic narrating, the standard world is unpredictably connected to the idea of the legend's excursion, a story prime example explained by Joseph Campbell. The legend's process ordinarily unfurls in stages, with the customary world addressing the underlying step. Campbell's monomyth frames the hero's takeoff from the standard, experiences with coaches and difficulties, and the possible return changed.

An exemplary illustration of the legend's process is found in J.R.R. Tolkien's "The Hobbit." Bilbo Baggins, living in the quiet Shire, is pushed into a phenomenal experience when he gets the unforeseen visit of Gandalf and an organization of dwarves. The Shire, Bilbo's conventional world, is pure and unsurprising. Nonetheless, the appearance of the call to experience moves Bilbo into a mission loaded up with mythical beasts, trolls, and the disclosure of his own mental fortitude.

Essentially, in Homer's "The Odyssey," the legend's excursion of Odysseus begins in the customary universe of Ithaca. The serene family life of his house is disturbed by the call to experience typified in the Trojan Conflict. Odysseus sets out on a risky excursion that takes him through the difficulties of legendary animals, help from above, and the preliminaries of character. The conventional world turns into ancient history as Odysseus goes through a groundbreaking odyssey.

The standard world likewise fills in as a story anchor, a perspective that permits crowds to observe the development of the hero. As the excursion unfurls, the unmistakable difference between the normal world and the exceptional difficulties amplifies the development, flexibility, and change of the person. This unique interaction is vital to the profound and topical reverberation of the story.

Think about the customary universe of Frodo Baggins in J.R.R. Tolkien's "The Cooperation of the Ring." The serene and rural Shire turns into an image of honesty and straightforwardness. As Frodo sets out on the unsafe mission to obliterate the One Ring, the customary world turns into ancient history.

The difficulties he faces, the fellowships manufactured, and the penances made highlight the significant changes in Frodo's personality. The normal world, when recognizable and safe, is perpetually adjusted by the phenomenal situation that develop.

In contemporary narrating, the standard world is in many cases described by its multicultural and various aspects. Creators and makers endeavor to mirror the intricacy of genuine encounters, implanting stories with a rich embroidery of points of view. This inclusivity extends the idea of the common world, embracing a horde of foundations, societies, and characters.

The customary world isn't restricted to a particular aspect; it includes the full range of human experience. It is a material whereupon the different stories of people and networks are painted. From the clamoring roads of metropolitan cities to the tranquil scenes of rustic towns, the customary world is a mosaic of human life, mirroring the bunch manners by which people explore their lives.

Moreover, the customary world fills in as an impression of cultural standards, values, and difficulties. It is a microcosm of the bigger social scene, reflecting the foundational designs and imbalances that shape the hero's excursion. From the perspective of the customary world, narrators can address and scrutinize social issues, welcoming crowds to ponder the more extensive ramifications of the hero's encounters.

In the investigation of the standard world, the job of optional characters becomes critical. Relatives, companions, guides, and foes inside this circle add to the lavishness of the hero's story. These characters, whether steady partners or adversarial powers, shape the hero's perspective, give direction, and catalyze the struggles that fuel the excursion.

Consider the standard universe of Scout Finch in Harper Lee's "To Kill a Mockingbird." The southern town of Maycomb, where Scout dwells with her family, epitomizes the racial pressures and cultural standards of the time. The associations with her dad, Atticus Finch, her sibling, Jem, and the baffling neighbor, Boo Radley, assume vital parts in molding's comprehension Scout might interpret profound quality, equity, and sympathy. The customary universe of Maycomb turns into the pot for Scout's ethical turn of events.

As the hero explores the common world, struggles under the surface frequently arise, adding profundity and intricacy to the story. Individual battles, questions, and inner strains increase the stakes of the excursion. This contemplative aspect permits crowds to observe the hero's inward change, giving a nuanced investigation of the human mind.

In F. Scott Fitzgerald's "The Incomparable Gatsby," the standard universe of Jay Gatsby is portrayed by lavishness, debauchery, and the quest for the Pursuit of happiness.

Notwithstanding, underneath the facade of riches and lavishness lies Gatsby's inner turmoil — a yearning for the impossible past represented by his affection for Daisy Buchanan. The common universe of riches hides Gatsby's interior longing, adding a layer of misfortune to his personality.

The customary world isn't just a story gadget however an impression of the human condition. It catches the recurring pattern of life, the interchange of routine and interruption, and the widespread journey for importance and reason. Whether in writing, film, or different types of narrating, the investigation of the standard world reverberates with crowds since it reflects their own excursions of self-revelation, goal, and flexibility.

All in all, the prologue to the hero and their customary world is a story foundation that grounds stories in engaging human encounters. It is inside this recognizable domain that characters become completely awake, molded by connections, challenges, and the commonplace schedules of ordinary presence. The common world is a dynamic and complex idea that stretches out past actual scenes to incorporate interior aspects, social scenes, and the different stories of the human experience. As heroes leave on their excursions, the normal world turns into a material whereupon the exceptional is painted, and the extraordinary odyssey unfurls. Whether in the domains of traditional writing, contemporary fiction, or speculative classes, the investigation of the common world enamors crowds by welcoming them to associate with characters on a profoundly human level.

**1.2 Something disrupts the status quo, a mysterious call to adventure.**

In the great embroidery of narrating, the disturbance of business as usual fills in as an impetus for story change, guiding heroes from the common into the uncommon. This crucial second, frequently encapsulated by a puzzling call to experience, goes about as the so-called inducing occurrence that pushes characters into strange domains, provoking them to defy the obscure, disentangle secrets, and eventually go through significant individual and aggregate changes.

The call to experience, covered in secret and charm, works as a story force that coaxes characters to step past the limits of their conventional lives. This mysterious request can appear in different structures — an obscure message, an extraordinary occasion, or an experience with a tutor or envoy. Anything its pretense, the call upsets the harmony of business as usual, giving heroes a decision: to embrace the obscure or grip to the security of commonality.

Think about the exemplary legend's excursion model, as expressed by Joseph Campbell. The call to experience is an essential stage in this story structure, arranged after the foundation of the common world. In fantasies and legends across societies, legends are coaxed by a baffling call that flags the beginning of their extraordinary odyssey. This call isn't only a plot gadget; it represents the widespread human experience of facing the new and the intrinsic craving for development, importance, and self-revelation.

In the domain of writing, J.R.R. Tolkien's "The Hobbit" represents the baffling call to experience. Bilbo Baggins, living in the peaceful Shire, encounters a disturbance of his standard life when the wizard Gandalf and an organization of dwarves show up unannounced. The call to experience comes as a journey to recover a lost realm and fortune watched by the mythical beast Smaug. The puzzling idea of this call lies in the obscure risks, the fantastical domains to be navigated, and the sheer daringness of Bilbo's takeoff from the solace of his hobbit opening.

Also, in J.K. Rowling's "Harry Potter and the Scholar's Stone," the baffling call to experience is unpredictably attached to the disclosure of Harry's mystical legacy. On his 11th birthday celebration, Harry learns of his status as a wizard and gets an acknowledgment letter to Hogwarts School of Black magic and Wizardry. The call to experience isn't simply an encouragement to go to an otherworldly school however a disclosure of Harry's actual character, his fate as a central participant in the enchanted world's battle against dim powers.

The puzzling call to experience stretches out past the domains of imagination writing into the texture of contemporary narrating. In the movie "The Framework," composed and coordinated by the Wachowskis, software engineer Neo encounters a disturbance of his everyday reality when he gets a puzzling message on his PC, teaching him to "Follow the white bunny." This apparently harmless call drives Neo to a progression of occasions that disentangle the deception of the standard world, uncovering a tragic reality constrained by man-made consciousness.

The baffling call to experience isn't restricted to the dream or sci-fi sorts; it pervades different account scenes. In Gabriel Garcia Marquez's "100 Years of Isolation," the town of Macondo encounters a secretive disturbance when a band of vagabonds shows up, carrying with them wonders and creations beforehand obscure to the occupants. This perplexing appearance denotes the start of the Buendía family's exceptional and wild adventure, disentangling throughout the span of 100 years.

The strange call to experience is in many cases epitomized by a tutor or envoy figure, somebody who has information on the obscure and fills in as an aide for the hero. This tutor, whether a savvy wise, a powerful being, or a guide with exceptional information, turns into a harbinger of the extraordinary excursion that is standing by. In old fantasies, figures like Merlin, the shrewd wizard, or Athena, the goddess of astuteness, frequently assume the part of coaches who start legends into the secrets of their missions.

Think about the secretive mentorship in C.S. Lewis' "The Lion, the Witch and the Closet." The Pevensie kin, living in war-torn Britain, are emptied to the open country. Lucy, the most youthful, coincidentally finds a closet that fills in as an entry to the enchanted place where there is Narnia.

Her secretive experience with the faun Mr. Tumnus makes way for the kin's call to experience, which at last includes the freedom of Narnia from the domineering principle of the White Witch. Mr. Tumnus, with his insight into Narnia's mystical domains, expects the job of a coach directing the Pevensie kin into the unexplored world.

In George Lucas' "Star Wars: Episode IV - Another Expectation," the puzzling call to experience comes as Princess Leia's trouble message conveyed by the droids R2-D2 and C-3PO. The coach figure, Obi-Wan Kenobi, rises out of the shadows of Tatooine to direct Luke Skywalker on an excursion that rises above the limits of the conventional. The call to experience is covered in the secret of the Power, the antiquated struggle between the Jedi and the Sith, and the predetermination that anticipates Luke.

The puzzling call to experience frequently works as a limit second, an emblematic intersection from the known to the unexplored world. This limit, addressed by actual entryways, mysterious gateways, or representative changes, highlights the significant change in the hero's excursion. It is a liminal space where the conventional world is abandoned, and the unfamiliar domains of experience anticipate investigation.

In Lewis Carroll's "Alice's Experiences in Wonderland," the puzzling call to experience happens when Alice follows the White Bunny down a deep, dark hole. The deep, dark hole turns into a representative edge, moving Alice from the commonplace truth of her sister's nursery to the eccentric and silly Wonderland. This puzzling progress denotes the start of Alice's strange and groundbreaking odyssey.

Essentially, in Neil Gaiman's "Neverwhere," the hero Richard Mayhew's common life in London takes a puzzling turn when he protects a young lady named Entryway. This thoughtful gesture drives him into the shadowy and fantastical domain of London Beneath. The edge second happens when Richard chooses to help Entryway and, in doing as such, leaves the security of his standard life for the vulnerabilities of a secretive and underground world.

The baffling call to experience is frequently interwoven with the subject of predetermination or destiny. Characters are brought into the obscure not simply by some coincidence however by an inestimable plan that sets them on a foreordained way. This feeling of fate adds layers of intricacy to the account, as heroes wrestle with inquiries of organization, choice, and the inestimable powers that guide their excursions.

In J.R.R. Tolkien's "The Ruler of the Rings," Frodo Baggins gets a secretive call to experience when he acquires the One Ring from his uncle Bilbo. This apparently honest piece of gems conveys a profound predetermination, as Frodo finds that he is the Ring-conveyor decided to convey the strong relic to Mount Destruction and obliterate it. The baffling call isn't simply an irregular occasion however a sign of a bigger predetermination that Frodo should satisfy.

In Sophocles' old Greek misfortune "Oedipus Rex," the hero Oedipus gets a puzzling prediction that predicts his fate. The prophet predicts that Oedipus will kill his dad and wed his mom. While trying to challenge this destiny, Oedipus unconsciously sets out on an excursion that at last satisfies the prescience. The puzzling call to experience, for this situation, is complicatedly connected to the unyielding powers of predetermination that shape Oedipus' heartbreaking life.

The secretive call to experience is in many cases joined by a need to keep moving, a ticking clock that prompts heroes to act quickly and conclusively. This criticalness adds pressure to the story, as characters wrestle with the results of wavering or deferral. Whether it's an approaching danger, a period delicate journey, or a quickly unfurling series of occasions, the secretive call requests prompt consideration and activity.

In Arthur Conan Doyle's "The Dog of the Baskervilles," Sherlock Holmes and Dr. John Watson get a puzzling call to experience when they are gathered to Baskerville Corridor to examine the demise of Sir Charles Baskerville. The desperation comes from the legend of an otherworldly dog that torment the Baskerville family, and the trepidation that Sir Charles' successor, Sir Henry, might be the following objective. The puzzling call urges Holmes and Watson to wander into the creepy fields and disentangle the conundrum encompassing the Baskerville revile.

The desperation of the baffling call to experience is clear in Beam Bradbury's "Fahrenheit 451." The hero, Fellow Montag, is a fire fighter entrusted with consuming books in a tragic culture where intellectualism is smothered. The strange disturbance happens when Montag experiences his insubordinate neighbor, Clarisse, who acquaints him with the universe of writing and decisive reasoning. The desperation lies in the severe system's crackdown on scholarly pursuits, moving Montag into a dangerous journey for information and opportunity.

Besides, the puzzling call to experience frequently requires an act of pure trust with respect to the hero. The obscure is overflowing with vulnerabilities, dangers, and likely risks. Characters should defy their feelings of dread, questions, and the appeal of the recognizable to set out on the extraordinary excursion that is standing by. This act of pure trust isn't simply an actual demonstration yet a mental and close to home acquiescence to the secrets of the call.

In J.M. Barrie's "Peter Skillet," the strange call to experience comes as Peter Dish himself, who welcomes Wendy and her siblings to travel to the mysterious universe of Neverland. The act of pure trust, for this situation, is exacting as the kids take off during that time sky with Peter. Be that as it may, the genuine jump lies in abandoning the security and consistency of their nursery for the marvels and dangers of Neverland. The secretive call provokes the youngsters to embrace the obscure and deliver their grasp on the standard world.

The puzzling call to experience is in many cases joined by a refusal or hesitance with respect to the hero. This underlying opposition is a characteristic reaction to the disturbance of the state of affairs and the vulnerabilities of the unexplored world.

Characters wrestle with questions, fears, and a hesitance to leave the security of the customary. The refusal is a story gadget that elevates the stakes, highlighting the greatness of the decision confronting the hero.

In J.K. Rowling's "Harry Potter and the Magician's Stone," Harry at first declines the baffling call to experience addressed by his acknowledgment letter to Hogwarts. The letter, conveyed by Hagrid, illuminates Harry of his status as a wizard and welcomes him to go to the supernatural school. Harry's hesitance comes from his doubt in his newly discovered character, as well as his connection to the Dursleys, his careless and non-mystical family members. The refusal makes way for Harry's unseen conflict and inevitable acknowledgment of the supernatural world.

In T.H. White's "The Once and Future Ruler," the youthful Arthur, known as Mole, at first declines the baffling call to experience when the wizard Merlyn uncovers his fate to turn into the future lord of Britain. Mole's hesitance is established in his absence of fearlessness and his impression of himself as a standard assistant. The secretive call moves Mole to face his frailties and embrace the phenomenal predetermination that looks for him.

The secretive call to experience, with its disturbances, earnestness, and difficulties, works as a story gadget that reverberates across societies and kinds. It takes advantage of the all inclusive human experience of wrestling with the obscure, defying predetermination, and exploring the intricacies of decision. Whether from the perspective of folklore, dream, sci-fi, or pragmatist fiction, the strange call spellbinds crowds by welcoming them to join characters on extraordinary excursions that rise above the customary. It is the coaxing power that drives heroes into the core of experience, where secrets unfurl, fates are uncovered, and the actual texture of the account is woven with the strings of the unexplored world.

## 1.3 The protagonist hesitates but ultimately decides to embark on the journey

As the baffling call to experience resounds through the story, the hero is confronted with a basic crossroads — the snapshot of choice. This vital decision, loaded down with vulnerability and the heaviness of likely results, turns into the support whereupon the whole direction of the story adjusts. The hero, having been disturbed from business as usual, presently remains at the edge of the obscure, faltering before the perplexing excursion that calls. It is inside this delay, this snapshot of examination, that the person's struggles under the surface, fears, and desires come to the front.

The dithering of the hero is an account pressure that adds profundity to the story. It reflects the innate human reaction to change, to the new, and to the difficulties that lie ahead. This delay isn't simply an emotional gadget yet an impression of the unseen conflict that goes with any critical choice. It is the wrestling match between the solace of the known and the charm of the secretive call — a showdown with oneself and an investigation of the person's inward scene.

In J.R.R. Tolkien's "The Association of the Ring," Frodo Baggins delays when given the obligation of bearing the One Ring to Mount Destruction. The heaviness of the ring's adulterating impact, the unsafe excursion that anticipates, and the apprehension about the obscure add to Frodo's underlying hesitance. This dithering is definitely not an indication of shortcoming however a demonstration of the gravity of the choice he faces. Frodo's inner turmoil is substantial as he wrestles with the greatness of the journey and the potential penances it involves.

Also, in J.K. Rowling's "Harry Potter and the Magician's Stone," Harry encounters wavering prior to choosing to leave on the excursion to Hogwarts. The disclosure of his enchanted capacities and the encouragement to go to the wizarding school challenge Harry's feeling of character and having a place. His faltering is established in the apprehension about the obscure supernatural world, the vulnerability of his place inside it, and the division from his existence with the Dursleys. Rowling breathtakingly catches the inner unrest of a youthful hero on the cusp of a life changing excursion.

Wavering frequently rises out of a feeling of dread toward the obscure, a trepidation that rises above the actual risks of the experience and digs into the mental and close to home domains. It is the apprehension about abandoning the natural, of going up against individual constraints, and of confronting the capricious spots of the excursion. This dread turns into an impressive foe, one that the hero should defeat to embrace the call to completely experience.

In Herman Melville's "Moby-Dick," Ishmael, the hero and storyteller, falters prior to joining the whaling campaign drove by Chief Ahab. The anxiety toward the obscure risks of the untamed ocean, combined with the unpropitious standing of Ahab and his resolute quest for the white whale, provides Ishmael opportunity to stop and think. Melville investigates the mental subtleties of faltering, depicting Ishmael's inward discourse and the possible choice to embrace the call of the ocean. The reluctance adds layers to Ishmael's personality, making his excursion all the seriously convincing.

The faltering of the hero is frequently weaved with a feeling of obligation or predetermination. While the call to experience might upset the conventional world, the hero's unseen fits of turmoil might rotate around tolerating the obligations that accompany the excursion. Obligation turns into a convincing power, encouraging characters to save individual bookings for everyone's benefit or the satisfaction of a higher reason.

In J.R.R. Tolkien's "The Arrival of the Lord," Aragorn wavers prior to tolerating his fate as the genuine ruler of Gondor. The heaviness of the crown, the obligation of driving the Free People groups against the powers of Sauron, and the feeling of dread toward flopping in his precursors' strides make a snapshot of struggle under the surface. Aragorn's faltering isn't a result of a craving for individual solace yet a significant acknowledgment of the penances and difficulties that go with his legitimate put on the high position.

The subject of obligation and fate is additionally obvious in Sophocles' "Antigone." The hero, Antigone, falters at the end of the day chooses to challenge Ruler Creon's pronouncement and cover her sibling Polynices. Her feeling of obligation to her family and the heavenly laws of entombment conflict with the natural regulations forced by Creon. The wavering isn't an absence of conviction yet an acknowledgment of the outcomes that her demonstration of disobedience might bring. Antigone's choice to satisfy her obligation turns into a terrible insistence of individual trustworthiness against severe power.

Besides, the dithering of the hero is frequently entwined with a moral or moral predicament. The call to experience might request activities that challenge the person's standards or power them to face moral dilemmas. This subtle conflict adds layers of intricacy to the story, as characters wrestle with inquiries of good and bad, equity and foul play, and the moral ramifications of their decisions.

In Fyodor Dostoevsky's "Wrongdoing and Discipline," the hero, Raskolnikov, falters prior to perpetrating the homicide that gets the course of the account rolling. The ethical predicament, the conflict between his philosophical defenses and the intrinsic feeling of profound quality, makes a significant struggle under the surface. Raskolnikov's dithering isn't simply an introduction to the demonstration however a focal component of the story that dives into the intricacies of human inner voice and the outcomes of violating moral limits.

The moral and moral components of wavering are additionally clear in Khaled Hosseini's "The Kite Sprinter." Amir, the hero, wonders whether or not to mediate while seeing the attack on his companion Hassan. The moral situation, established in issues of devotion, responsibility, and cultural assumptions, shapes Amir's way of living. The wavering turns into a vital crossroads that resonates all through the story, investigating the getting through effect of moral decisions on the human mind.

The choice to set out on the excursion, regardless of delay, frequently includes an acquiescence to the extraordinary capability of the unexplored world. It is an act of pure trust, an affirmation that development, self-disclosure, and change are tracked down past the limits of the customary. This give up is certainly not a detached acknowledgment yet a functioning decision to face fears, explore vulnerabilities, and embrace the intrinsic dangers of the experience.

In Imprint Twain's "The Experiences of Huckleberry Finn," the hero delays in any case chooses to set out on an excursion down the Mississippi Waterway. Confronted with the possibility of resisting cultural standards, facing racial biases, and exploring the intricacies of human connections, Huck Finn's faltering is obvious. Nonetheless, the charm of opportunity, the bond with Jim, the out of control slave, and the commitment of self-assurance impel him to throw away the shackles of his normal life and set out into the unexplored world.

This acquiescence to the obscure isn't elite to fictitious accounts; it finds reverberation, in actuality, excursions of investigation, disclosure, and self-improvement. People, when confronted with the call to experience, should wrestle with their own waverings, fears, and vulnerabilities. The choice to set out on another vocation, to investigate new societies, or to seek after an enthusiasm includes a comparable acquiescence to the extraordinary force of the unexplored world.

The idea of give up is distinctively represented in the genuine excursion of pioneer Ernest Shackleton. In 1914, Shackleton and his group set off on a mission to cross the Antarctic landmass, however their boat, the Perseverance, became caught in ice. Confronted with the obscure difficulties of endurance in the brutal Antarctic circumstances, Shackleton's administration became fundamental. The choice to set out on a hazardous excursion to look for help, leaving the security of the icebound boat, expected a significant acquiescence to the vulnerabilities of the frozen wild.

Additionally, the hero's choice to leave on the excursion is many times impacted by outside factors, like the consolation, direction, or intercession of guides, partners, or powerful powers. These outside impacts act as impetuses that steer the results, offering viewpoints, experiences, or backing that assist the hero with defeating their dithering and settle on the extraordinary decision.

In William Shakespeare's "Macbeth," the hero wavers prior to committing regicide however is affected by the heavenly predictions of the three witches. The witches' forecasts, combined with Woman Macbeth's consolation, go about as outer powers that drive Macbeth to embrace the call to desire and power. The choice to leave on the dull excursion is molded by an intermingling of inward and outside impacts, representing the mind boggling interaction between private organization and outer tensions.

The impact of coaches and partners is additionally clear in J.R.R. Tolkien's "The Master of the Rings." Frodo's choice to convey the One Ring is impacted by the direction of Gandalf, Aragorn, and different colleagues who perceive the size of the mission. The aggregate help of the partnership turns into a significant consider conquering Frodo's underlying dithering and imparting the boldness to wander into Mordor.

In contemporary narrating, the outer impact of coaches is investigated in J.K. Rowling's "The Lattice." Neo, the hero, at first delays prior to embracing his job as "The One," a messianic figure bound to challenge the man-made brainpower subjugating humankind. Morpheus, the tutor, assumes a critical part in directing

Neo through the dynamic cycle, testing his discernments, and opening his true capacity. The outer direction turns into an impetus for Neo's choice to leave on the excursion of self-disclosure and disobedience to the machines.

The choice to leave on the excursion, set apart by the hero's acquiescence to the obscure, frequently involves a representative or strict takeoff from the standard world. This flight is a physical and figurative passing of the boundary, an unequivocal step into the unknown regions of experience. Whether through an exacting excursion, an adjustment of personality, or an extraordinary journey, the flight implies the hero's obligation to development, investigation, and the unfurling story.

In Homer's "The Odyssey," the hero Odysseus delays prior to passing on the well-being of his home in Ithaca to join the Greek undertaking against Troy. The takeoff turns into an image of Odysseus' acquiescence to the call of courage, experience, and predetermination. His waverings and hesitance are not indications of shortcoming but rather impressions of the mind boggling feelings going with the choice to abandon the normal world.

The flight is likewise a common theme in contemporary writing, like in Gabriel Garcia Marquez's "100 Years of Isolation." The hero, Macondo, goes through a takeoff from its ideal starting points into a turbulent and mystical pragmatist scene. This takeoff denotes the change of Macondo from a customary town into an image of the recurrent idea of history, human undertaking, and the interchange of the real world and dream.

The emblematic flight isn't restricted to writing; it reaches out into different types of narrating, including film. In Christopher Nolan's "Origin," the hero, Dom Cobb, delays prior to tolerating a difficult task that includes entering dreams inside dreams. The takeoff into the domain of dreams turns into a representation for Cobb's acquiescence to the obscure and his excursion of compromise with his past. The choice to leave on this complicated mission is a takeoff into the dreamlike scenes of dreams as well as into the openings of Cobb's own psyche.

As the hero goes ahead into the obscure, the excursion unfurls with its preliminaries, adversities, and snapshots of disclosure. The choice to set out on the experience turns into a powerful power, impelling the story forward and molding the person's development. It is a guarantee to development, self-revelation, and the investigation of the obscure — a demonstration of the getting through charm of the call to experience. Whether the excursion prompts win, misfortune, or significant change, the hero's choice to wander past the standard world turns into a story foundation that reverberates across societies, classes, and narrating mediums.

# Chapter 2

**Crossing the Threshold**

The hero, having embraced the call to experience and explored the underlying ditherings, remains at the edge — the passage between the natural and the unexplored world. Passing this boundary is a representative and frequently exacting takeoff from the customary world, denoting the initiation of the groundbreaking excursion. This stage in the legend's excursion, as outlined by Joseph Campbell, is a crucial point in time that sets the hero on a direction of difficulties, disclosures, and individual development.

In J.R.R. Tolkien's "The Partnership of the Ring," the edge is encapsulated by the flight of the association from Rivendell. Frodo Baggins, alongside a different gathering of partners, passes the boundary into the unsafe domains of Center earth. The representative takeoff from the safe-haven of Rivendell, directed by the insight of Elrond and the partnership's mutual perspective, implies the start of their journey to obliterate the One Ring. The limit isn't only an actual limit yet a progress into a world loaded with risks, where the conventional standards never again apply.

Likewise, in C.S. Lewis' "The Lion, the Witch and the Closet," the limit is crossed when the Pevensie kin enter the enchanted place that is known for Narnia through the closet. The closet fills in as a gateway, a liminal space between the conventional universe of war-torn Britain and the charmed domain of Narnia. The passing of the boundary is a strict progress into an existence where talking creatures, legendary animals, and incredible fights anticipate. It is a takeoff from the wartime difficulties of their conventional lives into the fantastical and extraordinary scene of Narnia.

The idea of passing the boundary isn't restricted to the domains of imagination writing; it saturates different sorts and account customs. In Gabriel Garcia Marquez's "100 Years of Isolation," the edge is crossed when the vagabonds show up in the town of Macondo. The appearance of the vagabonds, with their wonders and developments, denotes the start of Macondo's takeoff from its normal presence.

The town goes through a change as it becomes laced with the enchanted pragmatist components that characterize the story. The passing of the boundary is definitely not a singular excursion however a shared takeoff into a domain where the remarkable interweaves with the customary.

The edge, frequently portrayed as a door, span, or temporary space, fills in as a representation for the hero's mental and profound change. It is a final turning point, where the explored parts of the planet disappears, and the unknown domains unfurl. The passing of the boundary is both a cognizant decision and an acquiescence to the unyielding draw of the experience that is standing by. It is the second when the hero ventures into the pit of vulnerability, moved by the call to experience and the commitment of development, difficulties, and disclosure.

In Homer's "The Odyssey," the limit is crossed when Odysseus withdraws from Ithaca to join the Greek undertaking against Troy. The common universe of Ithaca, with its homegrown serenity, is abandoned as Odysseus heads out into the huge and deceptive ocean. The passing of the boundary isn't just a takeoff from the solaces of home however a passage into the incredible odyssey that will test Odysseus' flexibility, sly, and perseverance. The limit, in this specific circumstance, is the limit between the known and the obscure, the homegrown and the gallant.

Also, the passing of the boundary is in many cases joined by emblematic components that support the hero's takeoff from the standard. Customs, services, or powerful intercessions mark this change, highlighting the gravity of the excursion and the groundbreaking idea of the experience. The passing of the boundary is certainly not an easygoing step however a significant commencement into the hardships that lie ahead.

In J.K. Rowling's "Harry Potter and the Logician's Stone," the edge is crossed when Harry sheets the Hogwarts Express at Stage 9¾. The demonstration of going through the captivated boundary between stages implies Harry's takeoff from the conventional universe of the Dursleys to the mystical domain of Hogwarts.

The excursion to Hogwarts isn't simply an actual progress however an emblematic passing of the boundary into a universe of wizardry, companionship, and predetermination. The ceremonial idea of this flight builds up the meaning of Harry's entrance into the otherworldly domain.

In T.H. White's "The Once and Future Ruler," the edge is crossed when the youthful Arthur, known as Mole, is changed into different creatures by the wizard Merlyn. This groundbreaking experience, a piece of Arthur's schooling, denotes the takeoff from the standard existence of an assistant to the uncommon fate of turning into the future ruler of Britain. The passing of the boundary is entwined with otherworldly components that reflect the significant changes happening inside Arthur and foretell the legendary excursion that looks for him.

The passing of the boundary is much of the time joined by an uplifted feeling of mindfulness and an acknowledgment that the common guidelines never again apply. The hero enters a domain where the laws of the common world are supplanted by the elements of the experience. This progress is a change in outlook, a reorientation of the's comprehension hero might interpret reality, and an acknowledgment that the excursion requests an alternate arrangement of abilities, viewpoints, and values.

In Lewis Carroll's "Alice's Undertakings in Wonderland," the edge is crossed when Alice follows the White Bunny down the dark hole. The drop into Wonderland is a dreamlike excursion where the customary laws of material science and rationale give way to unconventional and strange real factors. The passing of the boundary isn't just an actual drop however a reasonable flight into an existence where creative mind rules, and the normal requirements of the truth are risen above. Alice's consciousness of this shift is integral to the story's investigation of the fantastical and the silly.

Likewise, in Neil Gaiman's "Neverwhere," the limit is crossed when Richard Mayhew helps the harmed Entryway and is dove into the dull and fantastical domain of London Beneath. The customary principles of London Over never again apply as Richard explores an underground world possessed by otherworldly creatures and symbolic scenes. The passing of the boundary is a drop into the obscure, where Richard should adjust to the exceptional elements of London Underneath and face difficulties that resist the rationale of the common world.

The passing of the boundary isn't generally a smooth and consistent progress; it tends to be set apart by preliminaries, tests, or representative trials that challenge the hero's status for the experience. This stage isn't just about takeoff yet additionally about the hero's capacity to explore the underlying difficulties presented by the new climate. The edge turns into a proving ground where the legend's fortitude is inspected, and their obligation to the excursion is reaffirmed.

In J.R.R. Tolkien's "The Hobbit," the edge is crossed when Bilbo Baggins, alongside the organization of dwarves, wanders into the dim and premonition Mirkwood Timberland. The woodland turns into an emblematic limit, testing Bilbo's mental fortitude, creativity, and flexibility. The difficulties inside Mirkwood, incorporating experiences with monster bugs and the perplexing impacts of the captivated woods, act as preliminaries that get ready Bilbo for the more prominent risks that lie ahead. The passing of the boundary is definitely not a detached section however a functioning commitment with the difficulties that characterize the legend's excursion.

In addition, the passing of the boundary is frequently joined by experiences with edge watchmen — figures or difficulties that substitute the method of the hero's movement. These gatekeepers can take different structures, including guides, enemies, or representative snags that test the legend's purpose. Defeating these gatekeepers turns into a critical part of the legend's excursion, connoting their preparation to stand up to the difficulties of the experience.

In Arthurian legends, the passing of the boundary is exemplified by the entry into the magical place that is known for Avalon. Avalon is many times portrayed as a powerful domain, isolated from the common world by an enchanted hindrance.

The excursion to Avalon, whether embraced by Lord Arthur or other incredible figures, includes passing a boundary monitored by extraordinary powers. The emblematic guardianship of Avalon turns into a portrayal of the legend's preparation to leave on a mission that rises above the limits of the human domain.

The idea of limit watchmen is likewise investigated in contemporary narrating, as found in George Lucas' "Star Wars: Episode IV - Another Expectation." Luke Skywalker's passing of the boundary is set apart by his takeoff from Tatooine, directed by the coach Obi-Wan Kenobi. The edge watchman, in this occurrence, is the supreme bar that the Thousand years Hawk should avoid to leave Tatooine. The showdown with the bar turns into a trial of Luke's purpose and genius, making way for the cosmic experience that looks for him.

The passing of the boundary isn't exclusively an outer excursion; it is likewise an interior journey into the profundities of the hero's mind. This inside investigation includes going up against fears, questions, and internal struggles that might impede the legend's movement. The limit turns into a mirror mirroring the legend's interior scene, and the excursion is a groundbreaking interaction that reaches out past the actual domain.

In Hermann Hesse's "Siddhartha," the passing of the boundary is portrayed through the hero's takeoff from the conventional way of parsimony and profound unbending nature. Siddhartha's inner excursion drives him to a waterway, where he experiences the ferryman Vasudeva. The stream turns into an emblematic limit, addressing the smoothness of life and the interconnectedness, everything being equal. Siddhartha's takeoff from the parsimonious life denotes the start of a more profound inside venture, where he stands up to the intricacies of want, enduring, and the tricky idea of illumination.

Besides, the passing of the boundary is frequently connected with an adjustment of personality or a change of the hero. This transformation can be physical, mental, or emblematic, mirroring the significant effect of the excursion on the legend's being. The edge turns into an entryway to self-revelation, strengthening, and an acknowledgment of undiscovered possibilities.

In J.K. Rowling's "Harry Potter and the Logician's Stone," the passing of the boundary is interlaced with Harry's entrance into the supernatural world. The disclosure of his way of life as a wizard, the acknowledgment into Hogwarts, and the experiences with mystical animals mark the start of Harry's change. The passing of the boundary isn't just a takeoff from the customary world yet a transformation into a wizard, a significant change in Harry's character that impels him into a predetermination laced with the otherworldly domain.

The subject of personality change is likewise investigated in Suzanne Collins' "The Yearning Games." Katniss Everdeen's passing of the boundary happens when she volunteers to assume her sister Tidy's position in the Craving Games, a broadcast battle until the very end. The field turns into a representative limit, testing not exclusively Katniss' actual ability yet her strength, versatility, and moral convictions. The passing of the boundary prompts Katniss' development from a hesitant recognition for an image of opposition, featuring the extraordinary force of the legend's excursion.

Likewise, the passing of the boundary is much of the time joined by a disclosure or a developing comprehension of the journey's importance. This disclosure might come from coaches, extraordinary powers, or the legend's own experiences. The limit turns into a space of illumination, where the legend acquires clearness about their motivation, the difficulties ahead, and the stakes engaged with the experience.

In J.R.R. Tolkien's "The Partnership of the Ring," the passing of the boundary is combined with the disclosure of the real essence of the One Ring. As the partnership withdraws from Rivendell, Elrond confers information about the ring's malicious power, the dull powers that look for it, and the risky excursion ahead. The passing of the boundary isn't just a flight into the immense scenes of Center earth yet a significant comprehension of the mission's gravity. The disclosure turns into a directing light that enlightens the way ahead.

The passing of the boundary is an account model that rises above social and classification limits, reverberating across fantasies, legends, and contemporary narrating. Whether the excursion includes supernatural domains, legendary fights, or inward missions, the passing of the boundary is a general theme that catches the substance of the legend's excursion. It is the snapshot of takeoff, the inception into the obscure, and the impetus for change. As the hero ventures across the representative or strict edge, the experience unfurls with the commitment of difficulties, revelations, and the inflexible draw of predetermination.

## 2.1 The protagonist leaves their comfort zone and enters a new, unfamiliar world.

The hero's process takes a definitive turn as they abandon the solace and commonality of their conventional world, wandering into unfamiliar domains that hold the commitment of development, challenges, and significant change. This stage in the legend's excursion, frequently alluded to as the flight or the commencement, denotes a crucial second as the hero ventures past the limits of the known into the immense span of the unexplored world.

In J.R.R. Tolkien's "The Hobbit," Bilbo Baggins, a hobbit who esteems the peacefulness of his comfortable home, Sack End, is pushed into a surprising experience. Gandalf, the wizard, and an organization of dwarves show up, looking for Bilbo's help with recovering their country from the mythical serpent Smaug. Bilbo's takeoff from the Shire, the pure and quiet home of hobbits, represents the passing of the boundary into the risks and ponders of Center earth. His underlying hesitance gives way to a hesitant acknowledgment of the call to experience, making way for experiences with savages, trolls, and a definitive showdown with the winged serpent.

Essentially, in Suzanne Collins' "The Yearning Games," Katniss Everdeen withdraws from the recognizable Region 12 to partake in the Craving Games, a ruthless rivalry in a tragic culture. Katniss, who is talented in hunting and endurance, is pushed into the Legislative hall, a universe of lavishness and overabundance. Her takeoff from the devastated Locale 12 connotes an actual excursion as well as a change into a political and social field where she should explore the intricacies of the Games, unions, and the Legislative center's promulgation. The takeoff from her usual range of familiarity turns into a pot for Katniss' flexibility, versatility, and moral decisions.

Besides, leaving the safe place isn't exclusively an actual progress yet frequently involves a takeoff from the mental and profound wellbeing nets that characterize the conventional world. The hero defies internal feelings of trepidation, questions, and weaknesses, and the excursion turns into a cauldron for self-awareness and self-disclosure. This inward flight is distinctively portrayed in Hermann Hesse's "Siddhartha," where the lead protagonist sets out on a profound mission, abandoning the shows of his Brahmin childhood.

Siddhartha's takeoff from the otherworldly lessons of his local area is a significant inside progress as he looks for edification through direct insight. The takeoff isn't simply a dismissal of the known however a hug of the obscure, a giving up of the solace given by teachings and customs. Siddhartha's process turns into a single investigation into the profundities of selfhood and the intricacies of presence, outlining that passing on one's usual range of familiarity stretches out past actual limits to the openings of the spirit.

In contemporary writing, the takeoff from the safe place is much of the time portrayed as a reaction to a problematic occasion or a source of inspiration. In Khaled Hosseini's "The Kite Sprinter," Amir's agreeable life in Kabul is broken by the Soviet attack and later by the ascent of the Taliban. Amir's takeoff from Kabul to the US isn't just an actual break from the conflict torn city however a takeoff from the social, familial, and profound ties that characterized his conventional world. The newness of America turns into a proving ground for Amir's flexibility and a space for compromise with his past.

Moreover, the takeoff from the safe place is regularly joined by a coach figure, somebody who guides and helps the hero on their excursion. This tutor can take different structures — a savvy senior, an extraordinary being, or even an unforeseen partner. The coach's job is to give direction, support, and in some cases a push when the hero falters at the edge of the unexplored world.

In J.K. Rowling's "Harry Potter and the Scholar's Stone," Hagrid, the half-goliath maintenance person at Hogwarts School of Black magic and Wizardry, fills in as a guide to Harry Potter. Hagrid's landing in the Dursleys' home denotes the takeoff from Harry's normal life as a vagrant abused by his family members. Hagrid's direction stretches out past the prologue to the mystical world; he turns into a wellspring of help and support as Harry explores the difficulties and secrets of Hogwarts. The tutor's presence is vital in working with the hero's takeoff, imparting certainty, and forming how they might interpret the new world they are entering.

Besides, the takeoff from the safe place frequently includes an emblematic passing of a boundary or passage. This crossing connotes the hero's obligation to the excursion and the irreversible idea of their choice. In Lewis Carroll's "Alice's Experiences in Wonderland," Alice's entrance into Wonderland through the dark hole is an emblematic passing of the boundary. The excursion isn't just an actual plunge yet a takeoff from the guidelines and rationale of the normal world. The dreamlike scenes and fantastical characters she experiences become the scenery for her investigation of the unexplored world.

The representative edge is likewise investigated in Gabriel Garcia Marquez's "100 Years of Isolation." The appearance of the vagabonds in the town of Macondo fills in as a takeoff from the common, presenting mysterious pragmatist components that rethink the town's world. The passing of this representative boundary gets rolling a chain of occasions that length ages, molding the fate of the Buendía family. The flight turns into a story gadget that unwinds the normal and ushers in the phenomenal.

Leaving the safe place isn't generally an intentional demonstration; outer powers or conditions can move the hero into the unexplored world. In Yann Martel's "Life of Pi," the youthful hero, Pi Patel, encounters a constrained takeoff when the boat conveying his family and a zoo of creatures sinks in the Pacific Sea. Pi finds himself untied in a raft with a Bengal tiger named Richard Parker.

The takeoff from the natural universe of the boat is a horrendous mishap that pushes Pi into the boundlessness of the sea. The raft turns into a microcosm of the obscure, where endurance relies upon Pi's capacity to adjust and coincide with a considerable and possibly risky sidekick.

Besides, the new world that the hero enters is in many cases described by its unmistakable differentiations with the standard world. This differentiation features the difficulties and contrasts that the hero should explore. In Beam Bradbury's "Fahrenheit 451," the hero, Fellow Montag, withdraws from the abusive and hostile to scholarly society that consumes books. The new world past the limits of restriction and similarity is a scene of resistance, scholarly interest, and the quest for information. Montag's takeoff turns into a resistance to the solace of a general public that stifles decisive reasoning and a dive into a world that esteems the force of thoughts.

In Joseph Conrad's "Heart of Dimness," the hero, Marlow, withdraws from the natural universe of human advancement into the core of the African Congo. The takeoff is set apart by the actual progress from the External Station to the Internal Station, each step taking Marlow more profound into the unexplored world. The new universe of the Congo is described by its thick wildernesses, secretive ceremonies, and the unpleasant presence of Kurtz. Marlow's process turns into a plummet into the obscurity of human instinct, provoking his biases and driving him to face the ethical ambiguities of dominion.

The takeoff from the safe place isn't just an actual excursion however a mental and profound odyssey. In Fyodor Dostoevsky's "Wrongdoing and Discipline," the hero, Raskolnikov, withdraws from the customary universe of traditional ethical quality when he carries out a homicide. The takeoff isn't set apart by an actual movement yet by a plummet into the tortured openings of Raskolnikov's inner voice. The new world is certainly not a topographical area yet a mental scene where responsibility, suspicion, and existential emergencies become the territory of his excursion.

Besides, the takeoff from the safe place frequently involves a shedding of the old character and the presumption of another job or persona. This change is vital to the hero's advancement and their capacity to explore the difficulties of the new world. In J.K. Rowling's "The Detainee of Azkaban," Harry Potter withdraws from the Muggle world to join the enchanted local area as a wizard. His takeoff isn't just an actual progress however a change into a wizard-in-preparing. The recognizable character of a normal kid living with the Dursleys gives way to the freshly discovered way of life as an understudy at Hogwarts School of Black magic and Wizardry.

The subject of personality change is additionally investigated in J.M. Barrie's "Peter Container." The takeoff from the normal world is embodied by Peter Skillet, who drives the Sweetheart kids to Neverland. The takeoff isn't just an actual flight yet a takeoff from the limitations of adulthood. In Neverland, the youngsters shed their normal personalities and accept fantastical jobs, typifying the opportunity and creative mind of experience growing up. The takeoff turns into a festival of the groundbreaking force of imagination and the dismissal of the everyday.

Besides, the takeoff from the safe place frequently includes a showdown with the obscure, the strange, and the otherworldly. This conflict adds a component of vulnerability and wonder to the excursion, as the hero wrestles with powers past the extent of their normal comprehension. In H.P. Lovecraft's "The Call of Cthulhu," the hero withdraws from the standard world into the domain of astronomical frightfulness. The flight is set apart by experiences with antiquated religions, illegal information.

**2.2 Encounter with mentors or guides who provide insight and tools for the journey.**

The hero, having wandered into the strange regions of the new world, experiences tutors or guides who assume an essential part in molding their excursion. These guides, frequently having thinking, experience, or powerful capacities, become fundamental figures in the legend's account. Their direction gives understanding, confers critical information, and furnishes the hero with instruments important for exploring the difficulties that lie ahead.

In J.R.R. Tolkien's "The Cooperation of the Ring," Frodo Baggins, on his mission to obliterate the One Ring, experiences a few guides who become instrumental in his excursion. Gandalf the Dim, an insightful wizard, fills in as an essential tutor, giving direction and guidance to Frodo and the partnership. Gandalf bestows information about the set of experiences and force of the One Ring, the perils they will confront, and the meaning of their central goal. Furthermore, characters like Aragorn, Legolas, and Gimli offer their mastery and friendship, each contributing a special arrangement of abilities that will help Frodo on his burdensome excursion.

Tutors can take different structures, and in Suzanne Collins' "The Craving Games," Katniss Everdeen experiences Haymitch Abernathy, a previous Yearning Games victor, as her coach. Haymitch gives Katniss fundamental bits of knowledge into the complexities of the Games, methodologies for endurance, and important exhortation on exploring the political elements of the State house. His direction becomes critical in assisting Katniss with exploring the tricky waters of the field and adjust to the difficulties that emerge.

Besides, tutors frequently act as a wellspring of inspiration, motivating the hero to conquer hindrances and live up to their true capacity. In J.K. Rowling's "Harry Potter and the Alchemist's Stone," Harry experiences coaches like Teacher Albus Dumbledore, the insightful and kind dean of Hogwarts, and Teacher Minerva McGonagall, his Change instructor. Dumbledore, specifically, turns into a directing figure for Harry, offering intelligence, backing, and support. Dumbledore's faith in Harry's abilities imparts the certainty required for Harry to go up against the difficulties that emerge in his otherworldly training and his bigger job in the wizarding scene.

Coaches can likewise be eccentric and unforeseen, testing the hero's predispositions and catalyzing self-improvement. In Imprint Twain's "The Undertakings of Huckleberry Finn," Jim, the out of control slave, fills in as an impossible tutor to Huck Finn.

Notwithstanding the racial and cultural standards of the time, Jim grants significant life examples to Huck, testing his biases and offering direction on profound quality and human fairness. Jim turns into an ethical compass for Huck, impacting his choices and molding how he might interpret the world.

Besides, guides frequently have information on the extraordinary or magical components of the story world, furnishing the hero with apparatuses or capacities essential for their mission. In J.K. Rowling's "The Savant's Stone," Rubeus Hagrid, the Manager of Keys and Grounds at Hogwarts, assumes a pivotal part as a tutor to Harry Potter. Hagrid acquaints Harry with the enchanted world, gives him the way in to his character, and gifts him an incredible asset — the Radiance 2000 broomstick. This enchanted thing becomes a method for transportation as well as an image of Harry's thriving abilities as a wizard.

In Joseph Campbell's idea of the legend's excursion, the guide frequently presents the legend with a charm or a unique device that helps them in their journey. This charm, at times known as the "mixture" or the "aid," can be an actual item or a figurative portrayal of recently discovered information or power. Frodo's ownership of the One Ring itself in Tolkien's story fills in as both a weight and a charm —

an object of extraordinary power that, whenever obliterated, would achieve the legend's prosperity.

Notwithstanding the bestowal of devices, guides frequently furnish the legend with fundamental information that enables them to explore the difficulties of the new world. In C.S. Lewis' "The Lion, the Witch and the Closet," the youngsters who enter the enchanted place that is known for Narnia experience different coaches who grant vital data about the land's set of experiences, the White Witch's oppression, and the prediction of Aslan's return. Aslan, a grand lion and a strong tutor, offers direction on their journey to overcome the White Witch and reestablish harmony to Narnia.

The coach's job stretches out past simple direction — they additionally challenge the hero, pushing them to defy their impediments and empowering self-awareness. In J.R.R. Tolkien's "The Cooperation of the Ring," Aragorn, otherwise called Strider, fills in as a guide to Frodo and the partnership. Aragorn challenges the gathering, encouraging them to confront their feelings of dread and endure notwithstanding misfortune. His mentorship goes past the arrangement of information and instruments; it envelops the development of versatility and boldness inside the association.

Besides, tutors frequently have a profound comprehension of the hero's excursion, at times because of their own encounters or extraordinary experiences. In Homer's "The Odyssey," the goddess Athena fills in as a tutor to Odysseus. Athena, the goddess of shrewdness, helps Odysseus all through his excursion, offering key exhortation, masking him to support his movements, and interceding with different divine beings for his benefit.

Athena's direction comes from her heavenly insight, making her a guide who gives both pragmatic help and heavenly understanding.

The coach's impact can likewise reach out to forming the hero's moral system and moral decisions. In J.K. Rowling's "Harry Potter" series, Teacher Dumbledore turns into an ethical compass for Harry, directing him in exploring the intricacies of the wizarding scene. Dumbledore's impact shapes' comprehension Harry might interpret love, penance, and the significance of pursuing decisions lined up with one's qualities. The tutor becomes a wellspring of information as well as an aide in the improvement of the legend's personality.

Moreover, guides frequently act as a scaffold between the conventional and the remarkable, giving a connection to the bigger setting of the story world. In J.R.R. Tolkien's "The Hobbit," Gandalf goes about as a tutor to Bilbo Baggins, directing him into the universe of dwarves, mythical serpents, and incredible missions. Gandalf's information on Center earth, its set of experiences, and the approaching danger of Smaug the winged serpent assists Bilbo with understanding the gravity of the excursion he leaves upon. The guide fills in as an association with a more extensive story, assisting the hero with arranging their singular mission inside a bigger setting.

In Neil Gaiman's "American Divine beings," Mr. Wednesday, later uncovered to be the god Odin, fills in as a tutor to the hero, Shadow Moon. Mr. Wednesday furnishes Shadow with bits of knowledge into the presence of divine beings, their battles, and the fermenting struggle among old and new gods. Through Mr. Wednesday's mentorship, Shadow acquires a comprehension of the enchanted propensities that shape his general surroundings. The tutor turns into an aide in the hero's very own process as well as in unwinding the secrets of a world loaded up with divine beings and fantasies.

Moreover, coaches frequently encapsulate model characteristics that line up with the legend's requirements and difficulties. In the "Star Wars" adventure, Obi-Wan Kenobi and later Yoda act as tutors to Luke Skywalker. Obi-Wan grants his insight into the Power to Luke, directing him in dominating his Jedi capacities. Yoda, the shrewd and old Jedi Expert, assumes the job of a coach in Luke's later preparation. The two tutors typify the paradigm of the savvy sage, giving viable direction as well as profound and philosophical experiences.

In the legend's excursion, the tutor can likewise be a wellspring of motivation for the hero's self-disclosure. In Hermann Hesse's "Siddhartha," the hero experiences the ferryman Vasudeva, who turns into a coach and guide. Vasudeva grants astuteness about the waterway and life's repetitive nature, empowering Siddhartha to gain from the's stream. Vasudeva's mentorship turns into an impetus for Siddhartha's inside process, driving him to significant self-acknowledgment and edification.

Besides, guides frequently have an association with the otherworldly or mythic components of the story, rising above the impediments of the normal world. In J.K. Rowling's "The Detainee of Azkaban," Teacher Lupin fills in as a tutor to Harry, offering direction in the safeguard against dim expressions and assisting him with defying his feeling of dread toward Dementors. Lupin, a werewolf, typifies both the mystical and the emblematic, filling a the in as a guide hole between the conventional and the fantastical.

Notwithstanding their direction, coaches may likewise furnish the hero with a source of inspiration or a more profound comprehension of their motivation. In J.R.R. Tolkien's "The Master of the Rings," the wizard Gandalf fills in as a guide to Frodo Baggins. Gandalf not just gives fundamental information about the One Ring yet additionally grants a feeling of obligation and predetermination to Frodo. The coach's source of inspiration goes past simple direction; it imparts a feeling of direction that moves the hero forward in their mission.

Also, the coach hero relationship is dynamic and advancing. As the legend develops and faces difficulties, the tutor might go through changes or flights. In C.S. Lewis' "The Pony and His Kid," the talking lion Aslan fills in as a tutor to Shasta, directing him on an excursion of self-disclosure. Aslan's impact is significant, however as Shasta develops and faces his fate, the coach's immediate presence decreases, underlining the hero's confidence and development.

In contemporary writing, guides can likewise be depicted as imperfect or complex figures, adding layers to their relationship with the hero. In J.K. Rowling's "Harry Potter" series, Severus Snape, in spite of his adversarial disposition, fills in as a startling guide to Harry. Snape's intricate inspirations and activities become a wellspring of equivocalness, testing Harry and perusers ali.

## 2.3 Initial challenges and doubts emerge, testing the protagonist's resolve.

The excursion started with a murmur of vulnerability, as the hero wound up remaining at the slope of another experience. The air was thick with expectation, and questions waited toward the edges of their psyche like shadows declining to be dissipated by the illumination of assurance. As they left on this odyssey, the heaviness of the obscure squeezed upon them, and the underlying difficulties filled in as the principal trial of their purpose.

Exploring through the maze of uncertainty, the hero confronted the imposing foe of self-doubt. The irritating inquiry of whether they were really equipped for conquering the obstacles ahead cast a long shadow over their way. It was a fight battled not with weapons, but rather with the elusive defensive layer of self-conviction. Each forward-moving step expected a cognizant work to quiet the internal cynic that tried to sabotage their true capacity.

In the domain of the new, the hero experienced the eccentric territory of progress. Like a storm clearing across the scene of their life, change carried with it both tumult and opportunity. The anxiety toward the obscure appeared in the questions that reverberated through the passageways of their brain. However, in the midst of the choppiness, the hero found the versatility inside themselves, a constancy that could face the hardship and arise more grounded on the opposite side.

The excursion, be that as it may, was not so much as one. En route, the hero experienced partners and foes the same. Connections turned into the point of convergence of the account, every communication forming the direction of the unfurling story. The collusions manufactured in the pot of shared difficulties turned into a wellspring of solidarity, while the struggles tried the constraints of the hero's perseverance. In the transaction of associations, questions emerged about others as well as about the hero's capacity to explore the complicated trap of human feelings.

In the midst of the relational complexities, another layer of vulnerability arose — the equivocalness of direction. The hero wrestled with the existential inquiry of why they set out on this excursion in any case. The underlying clearness that prodded them right into it became darkened by the obscurity of disarray. Was it a mission for self-disclosure, a quest for a higher calling, or simply a break from the tedium of the natural? The responses stayed slippery, disguised underneath the outer layer of their awareness.

As the hero dove further into the maze of difficulties, the scene changed, reflecting the steadily moving nature of their unseen conflicts. The landscape of self-question gave way to the lofty bluffs of outside impediments. Each obstacle seemed outlandish, a transcending top that provoked the hero with the chance of disappointment. However, despite difficulty, they found supplies of versatility beforehand undiscovered.

The way forward was set apart by the deceptive waters of independent direction. The hero faced decisions that conveyed the heaviness of results, their repercussions reverberating through the texture of their excursion. Questions about the right game-plan turned into a constant sidekick, creating shaded areas over the intersection. The apprehension about settling on some unacceptable decision incapacitated them on occasion, taking steps to wreck the whole endeavor.

In the quiet between pulses, the hero tracked down comfort and contemplation. The snapshots of calm reflection turned into a shelter from the chaos of uncertainty that encompassed them. It was in these stops that they uncovered the internal compass, an aide that pointed towards the genuine north of their convictions. The questions, however determined, couldn't smother the glimmer of sureness that consumed inside, a fire energized by the unfaltering confidence in the excursion's motivation.

The hero's purpose confronted its most imposing test when gone up against by the apparition of disappointment. The feeling of dread toward missing the mark posed a potential threat, creating a long shaded area over the way they had track. It was a fight against the reverberations of insufficiency that resounded through the passageways of their brain. However, disappointment became not a decision but rather an educator, giving illustrations that braced their soul and enlightened the shapes of their personality.

In the pot of mishaps, the hero found the extraordinary force of constancy. The excursion was not a direct movement but rather a progression of pinnacles and valleys, each dunk in the territory filling in as a pot for development. Questions about their own versatility invigorated way to the acknowledgment that was not the shortfall of moves but rather the capacity to rise like a phoenix after rout.

The outer scene reflected the inner transformation, as the hero wandered into unknown domains of self-revelation. The questions that once restricted them became venturing stones, every one prompting a more profound comprehension of their own capacities. The excursion, it appeared, was as much about unwinding the layers of the self as it was tied in with overcoming outer difficulties.

However, as the hero climbed higher than ever, the air became more slender, and questions took on a subtler structure. The apprehension about progress murmured treacherously, addressing whether they were genuinely meriting the triumphs they accomplished. The inability to embrace success, similar to a ghost, tormented their victories, stirring up misgivings about the realness of their achievements. Achievement, it appeared, carried with it its own arrangement of difficulties — an interior milestone where the hero wrestled with the authenticity of their accomplishments.

In the embroidery of the story, connections assumed an essential part. The bonds shaped along the way turned into a wellspring of solidarity, yet they likewise tried the hero's capacity to trust and be defenseless. Questions about the goals of others turned into a repetitive topic, a shadow that lingered over each genuine association. The weakness expected to manufacture certified associations conflicted with the sense to protect oneself from possible disloyalty.

The hero, notwithstanding, discovered that trust was an extension that should have been crossed regardless of the gaps of uncertainty. The eagerness to broaden a hand, even notwithstanding past disloyalties, turned into a demonstration of their developing person. The excursion, it appeared, was an investigation of the outer world as well as a journey into the intricacies of human connections.

As the hero traveled through the parts of their odyssey, the underlying questions changed into a nuanced comprehension of the recurring pattern of life.

The story was not generally bound to a double of progress or disappointment however turned into a kaleidoscope of encounters that painted the material of their reality. Questions, once saw as enemies, became buddies on the excursion — a sign of the consistently present requirement for reflection and development.

The embroidered artwork of the account was woven with strings of versatility, self-revelation, and the perplexing dance among uncertainty and assurance. The hero, presently prepared by the difficulties confronted and the examples learned, remained at a vantage point, studying the immense span of the excursion behind them. The questions that once created shaded areas over their way presently showed up as far off reverberations, simple leftovers of the imposing enemies they used to be.

In the last parts of the odyssey, the hero wound up at a junction by and by. The street ahead, however natural, held the commitment of new experiences. The questions that waited were not a sign of shortcoming but rather a demonstration of the consistently developing nature of the human experience. The determination that had been tried and produced in the flames of difficulty stayed unfaltering, a signal directing them forward.

The excursion, it appeared, was a repetitive beat of difficulties, questions, and wins — an everlasting dance that impelled the hero toward self-revelation. As they embraced the vulnerability that lay ahead, the shadows of uncertainty were not generally dreaded yet recognized as essential to the excursion. The odyssey, with every one of its intricacies and vulnerabilities, turned into an embroidery of strength — a demonstration of the hero's faithful determination to explore the maze of life.

The hero's process unfurled as a tireless series of preliminaries, each test intended to investigate the actual substance of their purpose. All along, question appeared as a quiet enemy, hiding toward the edges of their cognizance. The underlying difficulties, similar to the initial salvo in an enormous chess match, looked to disrupt the hero, to measure the strength of their conviction. The way forward was covered in vulnerability, and the excursion turned into a pot where the hero's guts would be tried.

As the main strides reverberated in the immense territory of the obscure, the hero went up against the ghost of self-question. The irritating inquiry of whether they had the mettle to conquer the obstacles ahead cast a shadow over everything they might do. It was a fight pursued in the openings of the psyche, battled not with actual weapons but rather with the elusive covering of self-conviction. Every choice, each step forward, expected a cognizant work to quiet the inward doubter that looked to disintegrate their certainty.

The scene of the obscure ended up being an impressive enemy. Change, erratic and whimsical, turned into the hero's steady friend. The anxiety toward the new flourished, and questions grew like weeds in the fruitful soil of vulnerability.

However, in the midst of the mayhem, the hero found a natural versatility — a steadiness that could endure the hardships of progress and arise sound on the opposite side.

The excursion was not even one. Along the winding way, partners and enemies arose, forming the story surprisingly. Connections turned into a point of convergence, every collaboration a demonstration of the hero's capacity to explore the multifaceted snare of human associations. The coalitions produced in the pot of shared difficulties turned into a wellspring of solidarity, while clashes tried the restrictions of the hero's personal perseverance. Questions, both about others and about their own ability for compassion, turned into a repetitive topic in this many-sided dance of human elements.

Amidst relational complexities, another layer of vulnerability unfurled — the equivocalness of direction. The hero wrestled with existential inquiries, the actual substance of why they left on this excursion addressed. The clearness that at first energized their activities became clouded by the obscurity of disarray. Was this a journey for self-revelation, a quest for a higher calling, or a simple departure from the dullness of the natural? The responses stayed tricky, concealed underneath the outer layer of their awareness like antiquated relics ready to be uncovered.

The maze of difficulties changed as the hero ventured further into an unfamiliar area. The landscape moved, reflecting the intricacy of their unseen conflicts. Self-question gave way to the precarious bluffs of outer hindrances, every one seeming unrealistic, a transcending top insulting the hero with the chance of disappointment. However, despite difficulty, they found repositories of strength already undiscovered.

The way forward was set apart by the deceptive waters of navigation. Decisions lingered like great doors, every one conveying the heaviness of outcomes. Questions about the right strategy turned into a persistent sidekick, creating shaded areas over the intersection. The apprehension about going with some unacceptable decision incapacitated the hero on occasion, taking steps to wreck the whole endeavor.

In the peaceful minutes between pulses, the hero looked for comfort and reflection. These stops turned into a shelter from the chaos of uncertainty that encompassed them. It was at these times that they uncovered their internal compass — an aide pointing towards the genuine north of their convictions. The questions, however tireless, couldn't quench the gleam of conviction consuming inside, a fire energized by the immovable confidence in the excursion's motivation.

The hero's purpose confronted its most impressive test when stood up to by the ghost of disappointment. The feeling of dread toward missing the mark posed a potential threat, creating a long shaded area over the way they track. It was a fight against the reverberations of insufficiency resounding through the hallways of their psyche. However, disappointment became not a decision but rather an instructor, granting illustrations that invigorated their soul and enlightened the forms of their personality.

In the pot of mishaps, the hero found the groundbreaking force of steadiness. The excursion was not a direct movement but rather a progression of pinnacles and valleys, each dunk in the landscape filling in as a pot for development. Questions about their own versatility invigorated way to the acknowledgment that was not the shortfall of moves but rather the capacity to rise like a phoenix after rout.

The outer scene reflected the interior transformation as the hero wandered into strange domains of self-revelation. The questions that once bound them became venturing stones, every one prompting a more profound comprehension of their own capacities. The excursion, it appeared, was as much about disentangling the layers of the self as it was tied in with vanquishing outside difficulties.

However, as the hero rose higher than ever, the air became more slender, and questions took on a subtler structure. The anxiety toward progress murmured guilefully, addressing whether they were really meriting the triumphs they accomplished. The inability to embrace success, similar to a ghost, tormented their victories, stirring up misgivings about the credibility of their achievements. Achievement, it appeared, carried with it its own arrangement of difficulties — an inner milestone where the hero wrestled with the authenticity of their accomplishments.

In the embroidery of the story, connections assumed an essential part. The bonds shaped along the way turned into a wellspring of solidarity, however they likewise tried the hero's capacity to trust and be helpless. Questions about the goals of others turned into a repetitive topic, a shadow that lingered over each sincere association. The weakness expected to manufacture certified associations conflicted with the nature to safeguard oneself from possible treachery.

The hero, in any case, discovered that trust was a scaffold that should have been crossed notwithstanding the gaps of uncertainty. The readiness to broaden a hand, even despite past double-crossings, turned into a demonstration of their developing person. The excursion, it appeared, was an investigation of the outside world as well as a journey into the intricacies of human connections.

As the hero traveled through the parts of their odyssey, the underlying questions changed into a nuanced comprehension of the back and forth movement of life. The story was not generally bound to a twofold of progress or disappointment however turned into a kaleidoscope of encounters that painted the material of their reality. Questions, once saw as foes, became mates on the excursion — a sign of the consistently present requirement for contemplation and development.

The embroidered artwork of the story was woven with strings of strength, self-revelation, and the unpredictable dance among uncertainty and sureness. The hero, presently prepared by the difficulties confronted and the illustrations learned, remained at a vantage point, looking over the tremendous span of the excursion behind them.

The questions that once created shaded areas over their way presently showed up as far off reverberations, simple leftovers of the considerable foes they used to be.

In the last parts of the odyssey, the hero ended up at a junction by and by. The street ahead, however natural, held the commitment of new experiences. The questions that waited were not a sign of shortcoming but rather a demonstration of the consistently developing nature of the human experience. The determination that had been tried and manufactured in the flames of difficulty stayed immovable, a signal directing them forward.

The excursion, it appeared, was a recurrent cadence of difficulties, questions, and wins — a timeless dance that pushed the hero toward self-revelation. As they embraced the vulnerability that lay ahead, the shadows of uncertainty were not generally dreaded yet recognized as basic to the excursion. The odyssey, with every one of its intricacies and vulnerabilities, turned into an embroidery of strength — a demonstration of the hero's faithful purpose to explore the maze of life.

# Chapter 3

**Trials and Tribulations**

In the huge spread of time and the always developing woven artwork of presence, the human experience is frequently set apart by hardships. These difficulties, whether purposeful or push onto us by the impulses of destiny, act as cauldrons for self-awareness and flexibility. From the beginning of development to the current second, people and social orders the same have explored a bunch of obstructions, every preliminary transforming the shared perspective of humankind.

Quite possibly of the earliest preliminary looked by our predecessors was the determined battle for endurance in a cruel and unforgiving world. The crude human, furnished with minimal more than impulses and crude instruments, defied the considerable powers of nature. Cruel environments, savage monsters, and the consistent journey for food tried the constraints of human perseverance. It was in these cauldrons of misfortune that the seeds of versatility were planted, and the diagram for defeating difficulties was scratched into the actual texture of our DNA.

As developments arose and prospered, the idea of preliminaries went through a change. As of now not exclusively obliged by the prompt requests of endurance, people started to wrestle with existential difficulties that rose above the actual domain. The coming of coordinated social orders delivered another arrangement of afflictions — political struggle, social disparity, and the perpetual journey for power. The records of history are packed with stories of pioneers who adapted to meet these situations and the people who floundered despite affliction.

One such age of hardships unfurled during the archaic period. Feudalism, with its inflexible social orders and settled in power structures, made a scene where the ordinary citizens endured the worst part of cultural imbalances. Laborers worked perpetually in the fields, their lives entwined with the eccentric fortunes of their primitive masters. The Dark Demise, a staggering pandemic that moved throughout

Europe in the fourteenth hundred years, added an additional layer of enduring to a generally overwhelmed people.

However, in the midst of the obscurity, flashes of flexibility and development arose. The Renaissance, a social and scholarly development that expanded in the fourteenth 100 years, proclaimed a resurrection of human imagination and interest. Craftsmen, scholars, and visionaries rose above the constraints forced by their conditions, leaving a permanent heritage that would shape the course of history. The preliminaries of the archaic period, while considerable, turned into the pot wherein the blazes of human resourcefulness were aroused.

As humankind walked forward into the cutting edge time, the preliminaries going up against people and social orders took on new aspects. The Modern Transformation, a seismic change in the monetary and mechanical scene, achieved extraordinary changes. While it introduced a time of progress and development, it likewise brought about new difficulties — the double-dealing of work, ecological corruption, and the augmenting hole between the wealthy and the poor.

The twentieth 100 years, set apart by two destroying universal conflicts and the philosophical landmark of the Virus War, remains as a demonstration of the getting through limit of humankind to stand up to and conquer preliminaries of impossible scale. The revulsions of contention, the phantom of atomic destruction, and the battle for social liberties tried the ethical fiber of countries and people the same. However, inside the pot of affliction, developments for harmony, equity, and fairness picked up speed, reshaping the worldwide scene.

In the domain of individual preliminaries, the human experience is a kaleidoscope of delights and distresses, wins and losses. Connections, those perplexing embroidered works of art woven with the strings of adoration and friendship, frequently become pots of inner strife. The intricacies of human association, the rhythmic movement of kinships and sentiments, present difficulties that request strength, understanding, and split the difference.

Misfortune, a general and unpreventable feature of the human condition, creates a long shaded area across our way of living. The demise of friends and family, the disintegration of treasured dreams, and the unyielding entry of time all add to the woven artwork of misery that winds around its way through our reality. Notwithstanding such preliminaries, the human soul is tried, and the excursion toward recuperating and acknowledgment starts.

Individual personality, that confounding blend of nature and support, goes through its own preliminaries. The journey for self-disclosure, the battle for realness, and the cultural compels that try to shape and characterize us — all add to the pot of personality development. The preliminaries of understanding oneself and finding one's position on the planet are soul changing experiences that each individual should explore.

Emotional well-being, a vital yet frequently disregarded feature of the human experience, presents its own arrangement of preliminaries. The maze of the brain, with its exciting bends in the road, can turn into an overwhelming scene for those wrestling with uneasiness, misery, or other psychological wellness challenges. The shame encompassing emotional wellness issues adds an extra layer of intricacy to the excursion toward recuperating and self-revelation.

In the stupendous embroidery of human undertaking, the quest for information has been a consistent string. The hunger for understanding, the constant journey to unwind the secrets of the universe, has driven people to leave on scholarly odysseys full of difficulties. Logical transformations, outlook changes, and the conflict between laid out creed and historic disclosures have denoted the preliminaries looked by the people who try to push the limits of human information.

The hardships of the human experience are not restricted to the domains of the individual or the intelligent person. The aggregate preliminaries looked by social orders on a worldwide scale pose a potential threat in the contemporary period. The 21st century has introduced another arrangement of difficulties — the existential danger of environmental change, the intricacies of globalization, and the unpredictable dance among innovation and morals.

Environmental change, an emergency of remarkable extent, represents an existential danger to the actual texture of life on The planet. Increasing temperatures, outrageous climate occasions, and the consumption of regular assets messenger a retribution for humankind. The preliminaries of moderating and adjusting to environmental change require worldwide participation, imaginative arrangements, and an essential change in the manner in which social orders collaborate with the climate.

Globalization, while cultivating interconnectedness and reliance, has additionally delivered its own preliminaries. Financial imbalance, social conflicts, and the disintegration of customary personalities highlight the difficulties of exploring a world that is progressively interlaced.

The preliminaries of globalization request a sensitive harmony between embracing variety and saving the one of a kind social embroideries that characterize humankind.

Innovation, the situation with two sides that has impelled humankind into the computerized age, presents its own arrangement of hardships. The fast speed of mechanical headway, while opening additional opportunities and accommodations, has likewise raised moral issues and cultural worries. The preliminaries of exploring the advanced scene include issues of security, network protection, and the moral ramifications of man-made consciousness.

Amidst these preliminaries, the human soul perseveres, versatile and versatile. The examples gained from hardships become the structure blocks of intelligence, molding the shared awareness of humankind. The ability to defy difficulties, both on an individual and cultural level, is a demonstration of the persevering through strength of the human soul.

As we stand at the junction of the current second, the hardships that lie ahead are both overwhelming and promising. Our decisions, independently and on the whole, will shape the direction of our common process. The preliminaries of the past have shaped the forms of the present, and the preliminaries of today will manufacture the way toward a dubious future.

Notwithstanding preliminaries, the human experience is a demonstration of the persevering through limit with regards to strength, sympathy, and development. Every preliminary, whether individual or group, fills in as a pot wherein the substance of humankind is refined and refined. The embroidery of hardships, woven through the chronicles of time, recounts an account of persistence, development, and the unyielding soul that drives us forward into the unexplored world.

In the terrific mosaic of presence, hardships are not simple snags to be survived; they are the very filaments that give profundity and importance to the human experience. From the basic battles for endurance to the complicated dance of present day challenges, every preliminary leaves its engraving on the material of history. It is through the pot of preliminaries that mankind, with every one of its imperfections and goals, proceeds with its excursion through the tremendous field of time.

### 3.1 Series of challenges and obstacles that the protagonist must overcome.

Life, similar as an enamoring novel, frequently unfurls as a progression of difficulties and hindrances that request the hero's strength, mental fortitude, and genius. In this complicated story of presence, the human experience is described by a tenacious progression of preliminaries, every part introducing another arrangement of obstacles to be overcomed. These difficulties, whether commonplace or great, shape the personality of the hero, producing a story of development, self-revelation, and win over difficulty.

At the core of this account lies the widespread topic of individual difficulties — those private battles that characterize the pith of a singular's excursion. From the earliest phases of life, the hero fights with the test of self-revelation. The method involved with grasping one's personality, goals, and values is a twisted excursion set apart by reflection, investigation, and the route of cultural assumptions.

As the hero develops, the scene of difficulties grows. Instructive pursuits become an impressive territory to explore, requesting scholarly thoroughness, tirelessness, and the capacity to adjust to groundbreaking thoughts. The hero wrestles with the preliminaries of getting information, manufacturing associations, and graphing a course toward a future instilled with reason and importance.

Kinships and connections, those complicated embroideries woven with the strings of association, present another arrangement of difficulties. The elements of human connection, set apart by satisfaction, struggle, and the recurring pattern of feelings, impel the hero into a domain where sympathy, correspondence, and compromise become fundamental devices for exploring the multifaceted social texture.

However, woven into the texture of individual difficulties are the strings of outer obstructions that frequently act as cauldrons for character improvement. Monetary difficulties, cultural biases, and fundamental imbalances arise as considerable adversaries, testing the hero's courage and flexibility. These outside challenges, intelligent of more extensive cultural issues, highlight the interconnected idea of individual battles inside the fabulous embroidery of humankind.

In the more extensive setting of the human adventure, cultural difficulties frequently become the overwhelming focus as the hero wrestles with the intricacies of the world at large. The changes of history, set apart by wars, unrests, and philosophical conflicts, become the background against which the hero should explore. In these turbulent sections, the difficulties stretch out past the individual, enveloping whole networks, countries, and civic establishments.

One such age in the stupendous account of cultural difficulties unfurled during the twentieth hundred years. The world saw the frightening preliminaries of two universal conflicts that reshaped the international scene and tried the strength of countries and people the same. The phantom of contention, the pulverization created by viciousness, and the aggregate injury of a worldwide scale became characterizing components of a period set apart by phenomenal difficulties.

The consequence of The Second Great War introduced another arrangement of difficulties as the world wrestled with the real factors of an isolated Virus War period. Philosophical pressures, the atomic weapons contest, and the journey for worldwide strength made a pot in which the hero — addressed by countries and their chiefs — confronted the overwhelming test of keeping up with harmony and steadiness despite existential dangers.

The battle for social equality and civil rights arose as one more vital section in the adventure of cultural difficulties. The hero, in this occurrence, was not restricted to the lobbies of force yet reached out to the grassroots level, where people and networks battled against separation, disparity, and the disintegration of key basic freedoms. The Social equality Development in the US and closely resembling developments overall exemplified the victory of the human soul over dug in cultural impediments.

As the story unfurled into the last 50% of the twentieth hundred years, the difficulties took on a worldwide aspect. The ecological emergency, portrayed by issues like deforestation, contamination, and the exhaustion of normal assets, arose as an imposing foe. The hero, presently addressing the shared perspective of humankind, confronted the pressing test of safeguarding the planet for people in the future.

The 21st century carried with it another arrangement of difficulties that highlighted the interconnectedness of a globalized world. The advanced transformation, while bringing exceptional network and mechanical wonders, likewise introduced difficulties connected with protection, online protection, and the moral ramifications of man-made consciousness. The hero, presently exploring the mind boggling territory of the computerized age, wrestled with the quick speed of progress and the requirement for moral contemplations despite innovative headways.

In the background of these cultural difficulties, the singular hero kept on grappling with individual preliminaries that reflected and converged with more extensive issues. The quest for significant work, the mission for a healthy lifestyle, and the test of keeping up with mental and profound prosperity became vital strings in the embroidery of the human experience.

The aggregate difficulties looked by humankind additionally appeared in financial disturbances and international movements. Monetary emergencies, for example, the one out of 2008, uncovered the weaknesses of worldwide financial frameworks and tried the versatility of people and networks confronting joblessness, dispossession, and financial vulnerability. The hero, on a cultural level, wrestled with the repercussions of financial difficulties that resonated across borders.

Wellbeing emergencies, for example, the worldwide Coronavirus pandemic that grasped the world in the mid 21st 100 years, arose as a great preliminary for people and social orders the same. The hero confronted the double difficulties of wrestling with a lethal infection and exploring the cultural and monetary disturbances brought about by lockdowns and the stress on medical services frameworks. The pandemic highlighted the interconnectedness of the world and the basic for worldwide participation even with shared difficulties.

The ecological difficulties that had been approaching not too far off arrived at a basic point in the 21st hundred years. Environmental change, with its sweeping ramifications for biological systems, atmospheric conditions, and ocean levels, turned into an earnest and existential test. The hero, presently addressing a worldwide local area interconnected by ecological worries, confronted the overwhelming errand of relieving the effect of environmental change and progressing toward a more economical future.

The series of difficulties that unfurled in the 21st century provoked a reconsideration of cultural designs and values. Developments upholding for civil rights, value, and natural manageability picked up speed, testing settled in frameworks and requesting a reconsidering of the norm. The hero, both as an individual and as a feature of a bigger group, wrestled with the basic for foundational change and the overwhelming undertaking of destroying structures that sustained disparity and natural debasement.

As the story bend of difficulties and snags unfurls, the hero's process turns into a demonstration of the dauntless human soul. Every preliminary, whether individual or cultural, offers a chance for development, strength, and the development of shrewdness. The interconnected idea of these difficulties highlights the requirement for sympathy, cooperation, and a common obligation to building an additional impartial and manageable world.

Notwithstanding hardships, the hero — the individual, the local area, the country, and mankind all in all — leaves on a groundbreaking excursion. The development of character, the procurement of versatility, and the fashioning of an aggregate personality are the signs of a story that rises above individual sections to turn into an account of human tirelessness and the limit with regards to positive change.

The difficulties that accentuate the human experience are not simple obstacles but rather impetuses for development and change. The hero, confronting the back and forth movement of preliminaries, arises as a powerful power equipped for molding fates, testing standards, and defeating impediments that once appeared to be unconquerable. As the story of moves keeps on unfurling, the hero's process stays a demonstration of the getting through potential for win, flexibility, and the relentless soul that drives humankind forward into the unexplored world.

### 3.2 Developments in character, skills, and knowledge.

The excursion of life, much the same as a consistently advancing story, is set apart by a progression of significant improvements in character, abilities, and information. As the hero explores the perplexing story of presence, each experience turns into a cauldron for development and change. These turns of events, happening at the convergence of individual contemplation and outer difficulties, shape the hero into a diverse person whose person, abilities, and information develop couple with the unfurling sections of their life.

Character improvement, the unpretentious specialty of turning into the individual one tries to be, is a focal subject in the story of self-improvement. From the earliest phases of life, the hero wrestles with the basics of character arrangement. Adolescence, with its blamelessness and susceptibility, establishes the groundwork for ideals like sympathy, versatility, and interest. Early encounters, both positive and antagonistic, add to the chiseling of the hero's ethical compass and the capacity to understand anyone on a deeper level.

As the hero changes into youthfulness and adulthood, the intricacies of character advancement come to the front. The cauldron of character development turns into a point of convergence, as the singular wrestles with inquiries of self-disclosure, credibility, and the arrangement of individual qualities with cultural assumptions. The hero might stand up to unseen fits of turmoil, cultural tensions, and the consistently present journey for a feeling of direction, all of which add to the embroidery of character improvement.

Challenges, both individual and outer, assume a crucial part in forming character. Difficulty turns into a proving ground for strength, tirelessness, and the ability to endure the tempests of life. Whether confronting misfortune, mishaps, or the preliminaries of connections, the hero's personality is sharpened in the cauldron of involvement. It is through these difficulties that temperances like fortitude, empathy, and respectability are tried as well as produced into getting through features of the hero's personality.

The improvement of character is a progressing, dynamic interaction. The hero, similar to a stone worker refining their show-stopper, ceaselessly refines their personality through self-reflection, thoughtfulness, and a readiness to gain from the two victories and disappointments. The excursion towards turning into the best version of oneself includes a cognizant work to develop excellencies, dispose of indecencies, and explore the ethical intricacies of the human experience.

Lined up with character advancement, the story of life unfurls with the procurement and refinement of abilities. Abilities, the viable appearances of information and capacity, are the apparatuses that enable the hero to draw in with the difficulties introduced by the outside world. From the simple abilities gained in youth to the particular mastery sharpened in adulthood, the hero's range of abilities goes through a powerful development.

From the get-go throughout everyday life, the hero wrestles with crucial abilities that lay the preparation for future turn of events. Essential coordinated movements, language securing, and social communication structure the structure blocks of a prospering expertise collection. Instructive pursuits further extend this establishment, acquainting the hero with a different cluster of disciplines and developing mental capacities that act as the bedrock for further developed abilities.

The advancement of abilities isn't restricted to the scholastic domain; it stretches out to the domain of relational connections, the capacity to appreciate anyone on a deeper level, and versatility. The hero learns the craft of correspondence, exchange, and joint effort, abilities that are instrumental in exploring the perplexing embroidered artwork of human connection. Profound strength, the capacity to oversee pressure, and a sharp identity mindfulness become indispensable parts of the range of abilities.

As the hero develops, so too do the abilities expected to address the difficulties of adulthood. Proficient abilities, whether in specialized, imaginative, or authority areas, become the overwhelming focus. The cauldron of the work environment turns into a proving ground for critical thinking, direction, and the capacity to explore a dynamic and cutthroat scene. Versatility, an expertise sharpened through openness to different encounters, arises as a vital resource in a consistently impacting world.

In the story of abilities improvement, the hero frequently sets out on an excursion of long lasting learning. The quest for information turns into an impetus for expertise upgrade, and the hero gets new skills to remain important in a quickly developing society. The mix of innovation, the dominance of computerized instruments, and the development of a development outlook become fundamental components of the cutting edge range of abilities.

The crossing point of character and abilities improvement is especially clear in the domain of administration. Successful pioneers have a powerful range of abilities as well as show praiseworthy person qualities. Qualities like compassion, respectability, and the capacity to rouse trust are fundamental to effective initiative. The hero, whether driving a group, a family, or a local area, should explore the fragile harmony among skill and character to arise as a groundbreaking power.

Information, the third support point in the trinity of self-improvement, winds around its own complex account all through the hero's excursion. From the base journey for understanding in youth to the complex quest for specific information in adulthood, the procurement of information is a dynamic and ceaseless cycle. The hero, outfitted with interest and a hunger for understanding, sets out on a deep rooted odyssey through the domains of scholarly investigation.

Youth fills in as the underlying part in the hero's mission for information. The unquenchable interest of youth drives the investigation of the world, the scrutinizing of presumptions, and the disclosure of basic bits of insight. Instructive establishments become the pot in which the hero sharpens the essential information that will act as a framework for future learning.

As the hero advances through pre-adulthood and into adulthood, the journey for information takes on a more nuanced and particular person. Scholarly pursuits, professional preparation, and expert advancement become roads for getting mastery in unambiguous spaces.

The hero digs into writing, science, expressions, and humanities, looking to comprehend the intricacies of the world and the significant inquiries that characterize the human experience.

The computerized age, with its extraordinary admittance to data, reshapes the scene of information securing. The hero, exploring an ocean of computerized assets, should observe between tenable data and falsehood. Computerized education turns into an imperative expertise, and the capacity to combine data from different sources becomes fundamental in a world immersed with information.

The account of information improvement isn't bound to formal training; it reaches out to the domains of independent learning, experiential information, and the insight acquired through lived encounters. The hero turns into a long lasting student, embracing the way of thinking that each experience, whether victorious or testing, adds to a more profound comprehension of oneself and the world.

The crossing point of character, abilities, and information advancement is especially articulated in snapshots of emergency and change. While confronting misfortune, the hero's personality is tried, their abilities are put to a definitive test, and the information amassed over a long period turns into a reference point of direction. In these cauldrons of involvement, the hero goes through a transformation, arising with freshly discovered qualities, experiences, and a refined identity.

The amalgamation of character, abilities, and information arrives at its peak in the hero's capacity to contribute seriously to the world. Whether through proficient achievements, innovative undertakings, or demonstrations of administration, the hero turns into a powerful power fit for molding the story of their own life and impacting the more extensive embroidery of society.

In the great account of self-improvement, the hero's process is one of constant development, transformation, and self-disclosure. The interchange between character, abilities, and information shapes the story circular segment of a daily routine very much experienced. Each challenge confronted, every expertise sharpened, and every chunk of shrewdness acquired adds to the lavishness of the hero's story, making an inheritance that rises above individual parts.

The hero, furnished with an advanced person, a different range of abilities, and a broadness of information, turns into a specialist of positive change on the planet. The capacity to explore difficulties with effortlessness, to motivate and lead, and to add to the aggregate insight of humankind characterizes the pith of an embraced the hero excursion of self-improvement.

As the story unfurls into the obscure parts representing things to come, the hero stays ready for proceeded with development and advancement. The unique exchange of character, abilities, and information guarantees that the hero is certainly not a static substance yet a lively power equipped for adjusting to the steadily changing scenes of life. The story of self-awareness, a story woven with strings of strength, interest, and self-disclosure, keeps on unfurling, welcoming the hero to embrace the vast potential outcomes that lie ahead.

### 3.3 Introduction to allies and adversaries who play crucial roles.

In the fabulous embroidery of human experience, the story is definitely not a single excursion however a complicated transaction of connections, partnerships, and clashes. Vital to this perplexing story are the partners and foes who assume essential parts in forming the direction of individual and aggregate fates. Partners, with their help, fellowship, and shared objectives, give an establishment to strength and versatility. Foes, then again, present difficulties, trial of character, and open doors for development. Together, these characters advance the story, adding profundity, pressure, and subtlety to the unfurling adventure of life.

Partners, frequently depicted as close friends and compatriots, possess a unique spot in the hero's excursion. These people, limited by fellowship, familial ties, or shared values, become mainstays of help during seasons of win and hardship. Family, as the essential cauldron of connections, is in many cases the main wellspring of partners in a singular's life. Guardians, kin, and more distant family individuals offer an underpinning of adoration, security, and direction that shapes the hero's perspective.

Companionships, one more fundamental class of partners, acquaint a special dynamic with the story. Bonds shaped in youth, school, or shared encounters make an emotionally supportive network that reaches out past familial ties. Companions become associates in the excursion of self-disclosure, wellsprings of chuckling, and partners who give comfort during life's tempests. The variety of fellowships, from adolescence close companions to long lasting friends, adds to the extravagance of the hero's relational scene.

Tutors and instructors arise as coaches, offering direction, information, and intelligence. These partners, frequently possessing jobs in instructive or proficient settings, become instrumental in the hero's expertise improvement and scholarly development. Whether granting scholarly information, vocation exhortation, or life examples, tutors assume a urgent part in forming the hero's direction and adding to their own and proficient achievement.

Partners are not bound to the domain of individual connections; they reach out to the more extensive local area and cultural designs. Cooperative endeavors inside networks, whether nearby or worldwide, unite similar people making progress toward shared objectives. Social, political, or natural developments epitomize the force of aggregate activity, where partners join to impact positive change. The common vision, aggregate strength, and variety of abilities among partners add to the flexibility of these developments.

In the expert field, partners and colleagues become fundamental partners. The work environment, with its unpredictable trap of connections, requires coordinated effort, correspondence, and common help. Groups, driven by a typical reason, explore difficulties and celebrate victories together. The elements of expert coalitions contribute not exclusively to individual development yet in addition to the accomplishment of hierarchical goals.

While partners give an organization of help, foes acquaint a standing out component from the story. Enemies, frequently depicted as adversaries, bad guys, or deterrents, present difficulties that test the hero's personality, versatility, and capacity to beat obstructions. The antagonistic unique adds strain to the story, driving the hero to stand up to, adjust, and develop in light of outer tensions.

In private connections, clashes and conflicts inside families, fellowships, or heartfelt ensnarements make ill-disposed elements. These difficulties, while awkward, offer open doors for correspondence, understanding, and the goal of contrasts. Ill-disposed minutes become cauldrons for profound development, sympathy, and the development of compromise abilities.

In instructive and proficient settings, enemies might appear as contenders, contenders, or testing conditions. Scholastic contests, working environment contentions, and industry challenges test the hero's abilities, inventiveness, and strength. Foes in these settings act as impetuses for development, pushing the hero to outperform their cutoff points and take a stab at greatness.

On a cultural level, foes might appear as foundational imbalances, separation, or severe designs. Developments for civil rights frequently emerge in light of antagonistic circumstances, with people and networks joining against abuse. Enemies become the impetuses for cultural change, motivating the hero to advocate causes that rock the boat.

The division among partners and foes isn't generally obvious; people frequently possess the two jobs at various places in the account. Companions might become enemies during clashes, and foes might develop into partners through compromise or shared objectives. The ease of connections adds intricacy to the account, mirroring the powerful idea of human communications.

The transaction among partners and enemies is especially apparent in the political field, where collusions and clashes shape the course of countries and social orders.

Collusions between nations, driven by shared international interests or discretionary objectives, add to worldwide dependability and collaboration. All the while, international competitions, verifiable contentions, and philosophical contrasts make ill-disposed connections that can prompt international strains and clashes.

In verifiable stories, the jobs of partners and foes are exemplified through coalitions and clashes between countries. Universal conflicts, Cold Conflict contentions, and local struggles highlight the significant effect of international elements on the course of history. The connections among partners and enemies, whether conciliatory, military, or monetary, become critical in forming the predetermination of countries and the existences of people inside them.

The duality of partners and enemies is likewise clear in the domain of self-awareness. Unseen conflicts, self-question, and the fight against one's own restrictions make an ill-disposed unique inside the person. However, a similar individual, fully backed up by partners — whether coaches, companions, or family — can beat these unseen fits of turmoil and leave on an excursion of self-revelation and development.

The prototype legend's excursion, a story structure that rises above social and scholarly practices, frequently includes unions with tutors, guides, and partners who help the legend in their journey. All the while, the legend faces enemies, whether legendary beasts, outer difficulties, or internal evil spirits, that test their boldness and guts. The legend's excursion, a representation for the human experience, exemplifies the all inclusive topics of unions and clashes that shape the direction of individual stories.

The representative meaning of partners and foes stretches out to social and legendary accounts. In strict texts, legends, and legendary stories, characters structure coalitions with divine beings, spirits, or individual humans to defeat ill-disposed powers. These accounts, rich with original imagery, mirror the human mind's timeless battle with outside difficulties and the journey for amazing quality.

In the domain of writing and narrating, the characters of partners and foes are fundamental parts of a convincing story. Heroes, encompassed by a cast of partners, guides, and companions, set out on groundbreaking excursions that lead to self-disclosure and development. Adversaries, typifying difficulties, clashes, or restricting qualities, make pressure and drive the story forward. The fragile harmony among partners and foes is the pot where charming stories become fully awake.

The elements of partners and enemies are not restricted to the outer world; they additionally unfurl inside the internal scene of the hero's mind. Inside partners, like strength, self-assurance, and a positive mentality, enable the person to confront outer difficulties. Interior foes, like self-uncertainty, dread, or restricting convictions, present obstacles that require reflection, mindfulness, and self-awareness to survive.

The symbolic idea of partners and enemies stretches out to the domain of mental turn of events. Psychoanalytic speculations, like Carl Jung's idea of the shadow — the oblivious piece of the mind containing curbed shortcomings, wants, and impulses — feature the interior antagonistic dynamic. Incorporating and defying the shadow parts of oneself turns into an excursion toward completeness and self-realization.

The harmonious connection among partners and enemies highlights the intricacy of the human experience. Life's story is a mosaic of connections, joint efforts, clashes, and goals. The capacity to explore the mind boggling dance among partners and enemies turns into a critical determinant of self-improvement, strength, and the ability to contribute genuinely to the world.

As the account of life unfurls, the jobs of partners and foes develop, offering valuable open doors for reflection, variation, and change. The hero, whether an individual, a local area, or a general public, constantly wrestles with the steadily moving elements of connections. The interchange among partners and enemies turns into a ceaseless wellspring of strain, development, and the unfurling of a story that rises above individual stories to turn into an aggregate epic — the great embroidery of the human experience.

In the unpredictable show of human life, the job of enemies arises as a vital component, molding the story with difficulties, clashes, and open doors for development. Foes, frequently cast as bad guys or obstructions, assume a critical part in the hero's excursion, whether on an individual, cultural, or worldwide scale. Their presence presents strain, tests the versatility of the hero, and catalyzes change. As the story unfurls, the nuanced interchange among partners and foes winds around an embroidery that characterizes the shapes of the human experience.

On an individual level, enemies take on different structures, from subtle conflicts to outside clashes. Interior enemies, like self-uncertainty, dread, or restricting convictions, live inside the mind of the hero. These inward difficulties become impressive obstructions on the excursion of self-disclosure and self-improvement. Standing up to and conquering these internal evil spirits is a significant and progressing part of the human experience.

Outside enemies in private connections can appear as clashes inside families, fellowships, or heartfelt entrapments. Conflicts, contrasting qualities, and relational difficulties test the strength of bonds manufactured after some time. These struggles, however awkward, present open doors for correspondence, understanding, and the development of sympathy. The goal of outer antagonistic elements adds to the extravagance and intricacy of the hero's very own account.

In the instructive and proficient circles, foes frequently come as rivalry, difficulties, or hindrances to progress. Scholastic pursuits might include contentions for top positions, acknowledgment, or desired open doors. In the work environment, partners or contenders might arise as foes, making a cutthroat scene that requests expertise, flexibility, and key reasoning. Defeating these expert foes turns into a demonstration of the hero's capacities and potential for development.

In the domain of cultural difficulties, foes take on an aggregate aspect. Separation, fundamental imbalances, and abusive designs become considerable enemies that influence whole networks and underestimated gatherings.

Developments for civil rights frequently emerge because of these cultural enemies, with people and networks joining against fundamental shameful acts. The battle against cultural foes turns into an impetus for cultural change and the quest for an additional impartial and simply world.

International pressures on the worldwide stage embody the antagonistic connections between countries. Verifiable struggles, philosophical contrasts, and international competitions add to the perplexing elements of global relations. Ill-disposed collaborations between nations, whether political, financial, or military, shape the direction of countries and have extensive ramifications for the existences of people inside those countries.

With regards to verifiable stories, foes assume a focal part in forming the course of occasions. Universal conflicts, upsets, and clashes between countries become characterizing parts in the aggregate human story. Ill-disposed elements on a worldwide scale test the versatility of countries and people the same, leaving permanent engravings on the texture of history.

The metaphorical idea of enemies reaches out to social and legendary accounts. Legends confronting legendary beasts, divine beings testing humans, and amazing fights among great and evil represent the timeless battle among heroes and their foes. These original stories, resounding across assorted societies, mirror humankind's aggregate mind and the enduring subjects of contention and change.

In writing and narrating, the presence of foes is a story gadget that moves the plot forward and makes sensational pressure. Heroes face difficulties, stand up to clashes, and conquer snags introduced by foes, driving the story toward goal and character advancement. The abstract scene is loaded with notorious foes that have become images of strength, mental fortitude, and the victory of the human soul.

Mentally, the idea of the foe reaches out to the investigation of the shadow self. Carl Jung's thought of the shadow alludes to the oblivious piece of the mind containing stifled shortcomings, wants, and senses. Coordinating the shadow, defying one's internal enemies, turns into a groundbreaking excursion toward mindfulness, self-awareness, and the acknowledgment of one's maximum capacity.

The job of enemies isn't only to hinder or challenge; they act as impetuses for development, flexibility, and self-disclosure. Afflictions, whether inside or outside, brief the hero to dig profound inside themselves, taking advantage of repositories of solidarity and cleverness they might not have known existed. In confronting enemies, people track down open doors for change, learning, and the development of characteristics that characterize their personality.

The unique transaction among partners and foes turns out to be especially obvious while considering the double jobs people frequently possess in one another's lives.

Companions might become foes during clashes, and enemies might develop into partners through compromise or shared objectives. This ease of connections adds intricacy to the story, mirroring the developing idea of human collaborations.

In the political field, collusions and clashes between countries highlight the international enemies that shape the course of history. Strategic pressures, regional debates, and philosophical conflicts add to the complicated trap of worldwide relations. The connections between international partners and enemies have significant ramifications for worldwide dependability, security, and the prosperity of countries.

With regards to cultural difficulties, enemies frequently arise as fundamental shameful acts, segregation, or imbalance. Developments for civil rights, social equality, and fairness emerge because of these cultural foes. People and networks unite to challenge and destroy harsh designs, taking a stab at a more comprehensive and just society.

Monetary enemies, like monetary emergencies, financial imbalances, or worldwide financial slumps, have broad results on people and networks. The difficulties presented by financial foes test the flexibility of people and social orders, provoking the reexamination of monetary frameworks and arrangements.

In the domain of innovation and development, enemies might come as moral issues, potentially negative results, or the abuse of mechanical progressions. The quick speed of mechanical advancement acquaints difficulties related with protection, security, and the moral ramifications of man-made reasoning. Exploring these mechanical enemies requires a cautious harmony among progress and moral contemplations.

Natural foes, for example, environmental change, deforestation, and ecological corruption, present existential difficulties on a worldwide scale. The results of ecological enemies influence environments, atmospheric conditions, and the general prosperity of the planet. Moderating these difficulties requires worldwide collaboration, feasible practices, and an aggregate obligation to ecological stewardship.

The cooperative connection among partners and foes is apparent in the cultural reactions to emergencies. In the midst of misfortune, people and networks frequently meet up, shaping collusions to altogether address difficulties. Cataclysmic events, general wellbeing emergencies, or philanthropic crises highlight the significance of fortitude, cooperation, and the acknowledgment of shared mankind in beating afflictions.

The metaphorical idea of foes stretches out to social stories, where fantasies, legends, and fables frequently portray heroes confronting powerful or emblematic enemies.

These accounts act as similitudes for the human condition, investigating subjects of boldness, flexibility, and the victory of good over evil. The all inclusive allure of such stories mirrors mankind's persevering through interest with the original battle against affliction.

In the domain of self-awareness, the idea of confronting one's enemies takes on a significant importance. Self-awareness frequently includes going up against inward difficulties, beating fears, and exploring the intricacies of connections. Afflictions become open doors for self-reflection, contemplation, and the development of strength. The excursion toward self-completion is unpredictably connected to the hero's capacity to face and conquer individual foes.

The representative meaning of enemies stretches out to mental hypotheses, where antagonistic elements inside oneself are investigated. Mental social treatment, for instance, recognizes the job of negative idea designs as interior enemies that influence a singular's prosperity. The restorative cycle includes testing and rethinking these ill-disposed considerations to advance psychological well-being and strength.

The legend's excursion, a story model recognized by Joseph Campbell, frequently includes the hero confronting foes and beating difficulties to accomplish individual change. The legend, whether in fantasy, writing, or genuine stories, leaves on a journey that includes defying foes, going through preliminaries, and arising more grounded and savvier. The legend's process mirrors the all inclusive human experience of facing and rising above afflictions.

In the advanced age, the idea of online foes has acquired unmistakable quality. Network protection dangers, online misrepresentation, and computerized assaults present difficulties to people, associations, and countries. Exploring the computerized scene requires mindfulness, carefulness, and the advancement of methodologies to safeguard against online enemies.

The crossing point of individual, cultural, and worldwide accounts uncovers the interconnected idea of foes in the human experience. Whether in connections, cultural designs, or international scenes, the difficulties presented by enemies add to the intricacy and lavishness of the story. The capacity to explore, stand up to, and defeat enemies turns into a demonstration of the hero's strength, versatility, and limit with regards to development.

As the story of life unfurls, the jobs of partners and enemies keep on advancing, introducing new difficulties and potential open doors. The powerful interaction between these components shapes the direction of individual stories, cultural accounts, and the general human adventure. In confronting foes, whether interior or outside, people and networks find the profundity of their own assets and the extraordinary force of versatility. The story of partners and foes, woven into the texture of the human experience, stays a persevering and all inclusive subject that rises above individual stories to turn into an aggregate epic — the progressing and steadily developing story of mankind.

# Chapter 4

**The Abyss**

The void loosened up before him, a huge and endless gorge that appeared to oppose the actual texture of the real world. Its profundities were covered in obscurity, an inky darkness that gulped all light and left just the shocking gleam of far off, concealed sources. The air was thick with a harsh tranquility, broken simply by the far off reverberations of some inconceivable, supernatural presence.

He remained at the cliff, a solitary figure against the void. The ground underneath his feet felt shaky, as though the very earth itself shuddered at the edge of this grandiose void. He looked into the dimness, looking for any indication of what lay beneath, however the void offered no responses, just a feeling of premonition that gripped to him like a shadow.

As he looked into the void, recollections overflowed his brain - recollections of when the world was entire and the pit was just a far off legend. Yet, presently, it yawned open before him, an indication of the delicacy of presence and the dubious idea of the real world.

The excursion that had driven him to this second was a maze of exciting bends in the road, a labyrinth of hardships that had tried his actual soul. It started with a murmur, talk that discussed old bits of insight and secret information covered profound inside the void. It was a call that couldn't be disregarded, an enticing that pulled him unavoidably towards the edge.

He recalled the initial steps he took towards the pit, the vulnerability that distressed him with each propelling step. His general surroundings changed, transforming into a dreamlike scene that made no sense. Reality itself appeared to twist and bend, as though the texture of the universe was unwinding before his eyes.

The excursion was not without its colleagues - a diverse team of individual searchers who, similar to him, were attracted to the secrets of the void. Each had their own reasons, their own accounts that converged and veered in the tangled snare of destiny. Together, they wandered further into the obscure, exploring the slippery landscape that lay before them.

The void was not a uninvolved power; it was a no nonsense element that answered their presence. It tried them with deceptions that obscured the line among the real world and dream. Fantasies moved on the edge of their discernment, provoking their mental stability and driving them to face the profundities of their own feelings of trepidation.

However, as they dug further, they found that the pit was not only an actual void - it was an impression of the deepest openings of their psyches. It held a mirror to their spirits, uncovering the secret longings and most obscure privileged insights that hid inside. Each step carried them more like a retribution, a showdown with the shadows that stuck to them like a subsequent skin.

The excursion was not without its penances. En route, they lost allies to the pit - consumed by its unquenchable want spirits. The reverberations of their voices waited in the air, an eerie sign of the value that was paid chasing taboo information.

As the void unfurled before them like an immense embroidery of grandiose secrets, they experienced creatures that challenged portrayal - old elements that existed past the limits of existence. These inestimable divinities murmured secretive insights and puzzling predictions, uncovering looks at a reality that rose above human comprehension.

The gathering went ahead, driven by an unquenchable interest that verged on franticness. They confronted preliminaries that tried the restrictions of their perseverance, bewilders that necessary both mind and instinct to unwind. The actual texture of reality appeared to shred at the edges, and they addressed whether the void was a passage to edification or a plummet into franticness.

In the profundities of the void, they found failed to remember civic establishments that originated before the known history of the world. Remnants of old urban communities lay covered underneath layers of time, their designs a demonstration of the magnificence of developments tragically missing to the chronicles of history. The air was thick with the heaviness of centuries, and the walls murmured stories of failed to remember divine beings and infinite upheavals.

As they investigated the vestiges, they uncovered prohibited texts that discussed an enormous request outside the ability to grasp of humans. These texts uncovered the presence of infinite cycles, ages that rose and fell like the recurring pattern of tides. The void, it appeared, was an entryway to the actual heart of these vast secrets.

The further they dug, the more the limits between past, present, and future obscured. Time itself turned into a pliable power, bowing and bending because of the enormous energies that penetrated the void. They saw substitute real factors and equal aspects, each an impression of the decisions and activities that formed the course of presence.

In the core of the pit, they faced a definitive truth - a disclosure that rose above the restrictions of mortal getting it. It was a reality that discussed the interconnectedness, everything being equal, an enormous orchestra in which each note assumed a critical part. The pit, it appeared, was not only a void; it was the pot where the predetermination of the universe was produced.

As they remained at the nexus of presence, the limits among self and other broke down. They became channels of inestimable energy, vessels through which the base powers of creation and obliteration streamed. The actual texture of their creatures resounded with the grandiose vibrations that beat through the void, and they witnessed the immense embroidery of reality in the entirety of its multifaceted excellence.

However, with this disclosure came a significant comprehension of the delicacy of their human structures. They were nevertheless transient creatures, momentary sparkles in the grandiose territory. The pit, it appeared, held both the commitment of edification and the phantom of demolition.

As they arranged to abandon the void, they felt a feeling of appreciation for the excursion that had carried them to this point. The hardships, the penances and misfortunes - all were woven into the texture of their aggregate insight. They conveyed with them the heaviness of enormous information, a weight that rose above the limits of mortal comprehension.

The excursion had unavoidably transformed them, making a permanent imprint on their spirits. They rose up out of the pit with a freshly discovered point of view, a more profound appreciation for the secrets that hid past the cloak of standard insight. The world, when recognizable, presently appeared to be pervaded with a feeling of miracle and wonderment.

As they climbed from the profundities of the pit, their general surroundings moved and transformed again. Reality sunk into a similarity to predictability, yet the reverberations of their process waited in the openings of their brains. The void, however abandoned, kept on causing serious qualms about their impression of the world.

In the outcome of their excursion, they ended up wrestling with the subject of how to manage the information they had acquired. The vast bits of insight uncovered in the pit were both a gift and a weight, and they confronted the test of coordinating this recently discovered shrewdness into their daily existences.

Some decided to share their encounters, becoming harbingers of enormous insights in a world that gripped to the solace of obliviousness. They talked about the pit and its disclosures, winding around stories that rose above the limits of traditional comprehension. Their words, similar to swells in a lake, reverberated across the texture of the real world, contacting the personalities of those able to tune in.

Others, tormented by the heaviness of grandiose information, withdrew into isolation. The chasm had left scars on their spirits, and they looked for comfort in the peaceful corners of the world, wrestling with the existential inquiries that presently posed a potential threat in their cognizance. The inestimable embroidery, when a wellspring of miracle, presently bore the heaviness of obligation.

The excursion into the chasm had extended how they might interpret the universe as well as manufactured profound obligations of brotherhood among the searchers. They conveyed with them the common recollections of the preliminaries they confronted, the secrets they unwound, and the penances they made. The chasm, it appeared, had tried their singular backbone as well as bound their destinies together inseparably.

In the days that followed, the world at large remained careless in regards to the grandiose disclosures that had unfurled in the void. The everyday schedules of day to day existence proceeded, apparently immaculate by the significant insights that hid just past the shroud of normal discernment. Maybe the pit existed in an equal reality, stowed away from the look of the people who gripped to the wellbeing of the known.

However, the reverberations of the chasm resounded in unobtrusive ways. A gleam of acknowledgment passed between the searchers when their eyes met, a quiet affirmation of the common excursion that rose above the limits of communicated in language. It was a bond fashioned in the cauldron of the chasm, an association that challenged the imperatives of common connections.

As time streamed unavoidably forward, the searchers wrestled with the acknowledgment that their excursion into the void was nevertheless one part in the grandiose adventure. The embroidered artwork of reality kept on winding around itself, and they wound up trapped in the flows of predetermination. The chasm, it appeared, was not an objective but rather a waypoint on the unending excursion of presence.

The recollections of the pit turned into a wellspring of motivation for some, powering imaginative undertakings and inventive articulations that looked to catch the unspeakable quintessence of their vast encounters. Compositions, models, and works arose, each a demonstration of the significant effect of the excursion on the imaginative soul. The searchers became conductors for the grandiose energies that had flowed through the void, directing them into show-stoppers that rose above the limits of regular articulation.

For other people, the pit turned into a wellspring of reflection and self-revelation. The grandiose disclosures had uncovered the deepest openings of their spirits, and they set out on an excursion of self-change. They tried to adjust their activities to the enormous insights they had witnessed, endeavoring to live as one with the unpredictable rhythms of the universe.

However, notwithstanding the significant changes fashioned by the void, the world at large remained generally unaltered. Most of humankind kept on exploring the commonplace worries of day to day existence, ignorant about the enormous embroidered artwork that wrapped them. The chasm, in general, stayed a far off and extract idea, a legend that held no unmistakable importance to their ordinary presence.

As the searchers explored the flows of post-pit life, they wrestled with whether or not to impart their insight to the more extensive world. The grandiose insights were strong, fit for reshaping the actual groundworks of cultural comprehension. However, they likewise perceived the potential for misconception and double-dealing that accompanied such disclosures.

Eventually, they picked a center way. They became stewards of the enormous information, gatekeepers of the mysteries that lay past the cover. They framed a surreptitious organization, a general public of searchers who swore to safeguard the fragile harmony between the known and the unexplored world. They worked in the shadows, unpretentiously affecting the course of occasions to guarantee that the enormous insights remained protected from the people who might use them foolishly.

The pit, it appeared, had gave to them a sacrosanct obligation - an obligation to safeguard the delicate harmony of the enormous request. In the tranquil corners of the world, away from according to the unenlightened, they kept on investigating the secrets that waited just past the edge of discernment.

As the years passed, the searchers found comfort in the information that they were essential for a vast embroidery that stretched out a long ways past the limits of individual lives. The pit, when an overwhelming gorge, had turned into a wellspring of motivation and direction. It was an update that presence itself was an excursion, a steadily unfurling story in which every individual assumed an imperative part.

The pit, it appeared, was not a solitary substance but rather an impression of the grandiose powers that pervaded the actual texture of the real world. It existed in heap structures - in the profundities of the human spirit, in the immensity of the universe, and in the interconnected snare of presence that bound everything together.

As the searchers embraced the recurring pattern of life, they conveyed with them the illustrations learned in the pit. They explored the difficulties of presence with a newly discovered strength, directed by the inestimable bits of insight that had been uncovered to them. The chasm, however abandoned, stayed a consistently present impact, a steady indication of the secrets that lay just into the great beyond of customary discernment.

Thus, the enormous adventure proceeded, a timeless dance of creation and obliteration, of light and shadow. The searchers, as enormous drifters, traveled through the flows of time, abandoning a tradition of shrewdness and miracle. The pit, however concealed, beat behind the scenes, a quiet observer to the unfurling show of the universe.

Eventually, the chasm was an objective as well as an excursion - an excursion into the profundities of the obscure, an excursion that rose above the restrictions of mortal getting it. It was a demonstration of the limitless capability of presence, an update that the actual universe was a tremendous and complex embroidery ready to be investigated.

As the searchers embraced the consistently growing skylines of their infinite process, they comprehended that the chasm was an actual void as well as a representation for the unknown regions of the human soul. It coaxed to the people who actually thought about wandering past the wellbeing of the known, welcoming them to become planners of their own predeterminations.

Thus, the pit lived on - not as a simple memory but rather as an immortal presence, a timeless riddle that kept on forming the fate of the people who tried to unwind its secrets. The inestimable dance, it appeared, had no closure, and the searchers, similar to stardust dispersed across the huge field of the universe, embraced the boundless potential outcomes that lay before them.

As they traveled through the flows of time, the searchers conveyed with them the substance of the void - an update that, in the steadily extending embroidery of presence, there were in every case new boondocks to investigate, new bits of insight to find, and new secrets to unwind. The excursion, it appeared, was endless, and the pit was nevertheless a door to the vast marvels that anticipated the individuals who hoped against hope past the bounds of the known.

Thus, the enormous adventure unfurled, an orchestra of infinite energies that reverberated across the huge field of the universe. The void, when an overwhelming limit, had turned into an impetus for change, an entryway to the endless domains of plausibility.

The searchers, as vast explorers, cruised through the grandiose flows, directed by the reverberations of the chasm that waited in the openings of their shared mindset.

In the excellent embroidery of presence, the void was nevertheless one string - a string that wove together the tales of endless grandiose drifters who had thought for even a moment to wander into the unexplored world. The searchers, limited by a common fate, pushed ahead with a feeling of direction and respect for the secrets that lay ahead. The chasm, it appeared, was an objective as well as a ceaseless excursion into the boundless profundities of the vast unexplored world.

### 4.1 The protagonist faces a major setback or crisis.

Life had been a progression of recurring patterns for Alex, a cadence of wins and difficulties that molded the story of their reality. In the calm corners of their heart, they held onto dreams and yearnings, energized by a constant assurance to cut a significant way through the immense breadth of potential outcomes. Nonetheless, destiny, in its impulsive dance, organized an ensemble of occasions that would before long push Alex into the wild profundities of an emergency that resounded through the actual center of their being.

It started harmlessly enough - a promising vocation, an organization of strong companions, and a feeling of direction that moved them forward. However, as the wheel of time turned, unexpected conditions unfurled, winding around an embroidery of difficulty that tried the fortitude of their flexibility. The primary difficult situations arose on the expert front, as the organization they had committed a long time to went through a seismic change in administration and course.

The once-steady ground underneath Alex's feet started to tremble as cutbacks undulated through the association. The air in the workplace turned out to be thick with vulnerability, and murmurs of rebuilding and cutting back reverberated in the lobbies. Nervousness held Alex, as they understood that the tides of progress were unavoidably clearing away the steadiness they had constructed fastidiously throughout the long term.

The emergency arrived at its apex when the unavoidable occurred - the declaration of huge cutbacks that sent shockwaves through the labor force. The once-recognizable appearances of partners currently bore articulations of tension and dread, as everybody wrestled with the unexpected disturbance that undermined their livelihoods. Alex, as well, tracked down their name on the rundown of those considered disposable in the heartless math of corporate rebuilding.

The news hit like a demolition hammer, breaking the deception of safety that had covered them for such a long time. Influxes of doubt and outrage ran into the shores of their cognizance, abandoning a destruction of run trusts and broke assumptions. The work, when a wellspring of satisfaction and reason, had turned into a setback in the unpredictable scene of corporate unpredictability.

In the days that followed, Alex explored the dreamlike course of getting out their work area - a custom that felt like an untimely memorial service for a part of their life that had finished suddenly. Associates offered thoughtful looks and reassuring words, however the sting of double-crossing waited in the air. The end was not an impression of their capacities or commitment, but instead a setback from conditions outside of their reach.

The emergency stretched out past the expert domain, saturating different features of Alex's life like a treacherous toxin. The monetary ramifications of joblessness cast a long, foreboding shadow over their future. Home loans, bills, and obligations posed a potential threat, taking steps to squash them under the heaviness of a dubious tomorrow. The security net they had accepted to be strong had unwound, allowing them to remain uncovered to the unforgiving breezes of financial unsteadiness.

As the days transformed into weeks, the emergency extended, and Alex wound up wrestling with outside difficulties as well as with the inside unrest of character and reason. The occupation had been something other than a method for making money; it had been a foundation of their personality, a wellspring of pride and satisfaction. Deprived of this job, they felt loose, a boat without a compass in the turbulent oceans of vulnerability.

The emergency turned into a cauldron, testing their monetary flexibility as well as their profound and mental guts. Restless evenings were interspersed by the incessant murmur of uneasiness, a determined friend that murmured most pessimistic scenario situations and self-uncertainty into the openings of their cognizance. The future, when a material of limitless open doors, presently showed up as a premonition scene loaded with deterrents and traps.

Amidst this disturbance, Alex looked for comfort in the help of loved ones. The strength of their social bonds turned into a life saver, a wellspring of close to home food in a period of significant weakness. However, even in the midst of the consoling hugs and encouraging words, a biting insecurity waited. The emergency had shaken their outside world as well as uncovered the delicacy of their healthy identity worth.

The quest for new business turned into a steady pursuit, a long distance race of utilizations, meetings, and dismissals that tried the perseverance of their soul. Every dismissal letter felt like a knife to the heart, a substantial sign of the difficult task they looked in recovering a feeling of business as usual. The work market, once safe with certainty, presently appeared as though an invulnerable fort protected by unfavorable difficulties.

The emergency transformed into an excursion of self-revelation, as Alex faced the awkward insights that lay underneath the outer layer of their cognizance. The quest for outside approval through vocation achievement gave way to a more profound reflection, a journey to uncover the interests and values that characterized their most genuine self. In the pot of misfortune, they tracked down a chance for reevaluation, an opportunity to reclassify accomplishment according to their own preferences.

As the weeks transformed into months, a similarity to versatility arose inside Alex. The emergency, however distant from over, had turned into an extraordinary power, an impetus for development and self-restoration. They embraced the inconvenience of vulnerability, remembering it as a ripe ground for the seeds of individual development. The quest for a new position became a method for monetary steadiness as well as an excursion towards adjusting their expert interests to their genuine self.

In the isolation of self-reflection, Alex reconsidered their needs and desires. The emergency had stripped away the unessential layers of cultural assumptions, uncovering the center of their actual longings. It was a retribution with credibility, a course of shedding the covers of similarity and embracing the unvarnished reality of their own goals.

The excursion towards self-reevaluation was not without its mishaps. The work market stayed a considerable enemy, and dismissal turned into a steady friend. However, with every misfortune, Alex found repositories of flexibility they never knew existed. The emergency, when seen as an inconceivable impediment, turned into a venturing stone towards a more genuine and reason driven presence.

In the maze of reexamination, Alex tracked down startling partners - tutors who offered direction, valuable open doors that rose up out of the unlikeliest of sources, and a local area of similar people exploring comparative excursions. The emergency, it appeared, had produced associations that rose above the shallow limits of expert affiliations. Together, they shaped an organization of common help, sharing bits of knowledge and consolation even with shared difficulties.

The emergency, however excruciating, had turned into an instructor. It granted illustrations of versatility, strength, and the significance of developing an inward locus of control. The outer conditions, when tyrants of their close to home scene, presently assumed a lower priority in relation to the inward wellspring of solidarity and assurance that had been uncovered in the pot of misfortune.

As the tides of progress proceeded to recurring pattern, Alex discovered a recharged feeling of direction that rose above the bounds of a conventional vocation way. The emergency had catalyzed a change in outlook, driving them towards tries that adjusted all the more truly with their interests and values. Pioneering adventures, imaginative pursuits, and local area drives became central marks of their excursion, each a demonstration of the strength and versatility that had bloomed following emergency.

The emergency, it appeared, had shaped a phoenix from the cinders of their previous self. The story of exploitation gave way to one of strengthening and organization. Alex embraced the vulnerability representing things to come not with fear, but rather with a feeling of experience, perceiving that the actual excursion was essentially as critical as the objective.

In the embroidery of their life, the emergency turned into a characterizing string - a string that additional profundity and intricacy to the story of their reality. The misfortunes, however excruciating, became venturing stones towards a more valid and satisfying life. The quest for progress changed from an outer approval to a sense of direction, directing them towards tries that resounded with the substance of what their identity was.

As the emergency progressively retreated into the chronicles of their past, Alex remained on the incline of another section. The injuries of the trial had recuperated, abandoning scars that gave testimony regarding the groundbreaking excursion they had embraced. The expert mishaps, however huge, had become impetuses for self-improvement, versatility, and the revelation of an unshakeable identity.

The emergency, in its wild wake, had turned into an impetus for a more significant comprehension of life's temporariness and the strength of the human soul. Alex, once fastened to the deception of steadiness, had figured out how to move in the downpour of vulnerability, embracing the magnificence of the capricious beat that formed the orchestra of their reality.

The emergency, however an imposing foe, had turned into a surprising partner. It had untethered Alex from the wellbeing of the known, moving them into the unfamiliar region of self-disclosure and reexamination. The excursion, however challenging, had turned into a demonstration of the dauntless soul that lived inside each person - a soul that could face the hardships of emergency and arise more grounded on the opposite side.

Thus, as Alex looked into the distance of the obscure, they did as such with a recently discovered feeling of appreciation for the emergency that had re-imagined the scene of their life. The difficulties, however excruciating, had turned into the prolific soil from which the seeds of strength and realness had bloomed. The emergency, when seen as an enemy.

**4.2 A moment of profound self-discovery and transformation.**

Life had consistently unfurled for Sarah like a wandering stream, its ebbs and flows directing her through the different scenes of involvement. However, in the midst of the undulating venture, there came a second — a urgent second that would scratch itself into the texture of her reality, changing the direction of the waterway and reshaping the actual shapes of her personality. It was a snapshot of significant self-disclosure, an enlivening that undulated through the profundities of her spirit and coaxed her towards an extraordinary odyssey.

The impetus for this transformation was an unforeseen and bumping episode — an individual misfortune that broke the deception of strength that had covered Sarah for such a long time. The passing of a friend or family member, a spirit shaking takeoff, turned into the seismic power that aired out the facade of her regular reality, uncovering the crude and weak center underneath.

In the consequence of this significant misfortune, Sarah wound up exploring the maze of despondency, a landscape new and muddling. The feelings, as stormy waves, took steps to inundate her, maneuvering her into the profundities of distress. However, inside the tumult, a glint of mindfulness lighted — a flash that would before long blast into the groundbreaking flares of self-disclosure.

The excursion into self-revelation was not a straight way but rather a circumlocutory investigation of the deepest openings of her being. Sarah dug into the intricacies of her feelings, permitting the rushes of melancholy to wash over her like a soothing tide. She defied the bunch features of misfortune — the throb of nonattendance, the reverberations of implicit words, and the frightful presence of what would never be.

As the days transformed into weeks, Sarah found a startling sidekick inside the profundities of her distress — strength. The actual center of her being, once compromised with disintegration, uncovered an innate strength that challenged the heaviness of distress. It was a strength conceived not from opposition but rather from acknowledgment — an eagerness to embrace the aggravation and permit it to shape the forms of her developing character.

In the isolation of contemplation, Sarah set out on an excursion of self-reflection. She returned to the stories of her past, investigating the perplexing strings of her encounters that had woven the embroidered artwork of her current self. The misfortune, however intensely difficult, turned into an impetus for a more profound comprehension of the perplexing trap of associations that characterized her connections, her qualities, and the actual substance of her reality.

Amidst this significant self-investigation, Sarah coincidentally found a disclosure — a revelation that rose above the limits of melancholy. She understood that the embodiment of her personality was not exclusively characterized by outer jobs or connections. Rather, it was a complex mosaic molded by her convictions, goals, and the manner in which she decided to explore the woven artwork of life.

This acknowledgment denoted a defining moment — a snapshot of resurrection that pushed Sarah towards an extraordinary excursion of self-completion. It was as of now not tied in with gripping to the parts of the past or surrendering to the heaviness of melancholy. All things considered, it turned into a journey to uncover the credible self — the self that existed past the bounds of cultural assumptions and outside approvals.

The excursion towards self-disclosure took surprising structures. Sarah dug into new encounters, venturing outside the safe places that had once characterized the boundaries of her reality. She embraced the obscure, permitting the new scenes of life to shape how she might interpret self. Simultaneously, she found lethargic interests and neglected aspects of her character that had extended remained clouded.

Innovativeness turned into a course for self-articulation. In the peaceful hours, Sarah tracked down comfort in imaginative pursuits — painting, composing, and making. The material turned into a mirror mirroring the kaleidoscope of her feelings, and the composed word turned into a soothing delivery for the contemplations that whirled inside the openings of her psyche. The inventive strategy, when a far off colleague, turned into a close partner in the excursion towards self-revelation.

In the midst of the outside investigations, Sarah additionally dug into the profundities of her conviction frameworks and values. She scrutinized the stories that had been given over through ages and investigated the cultural assumptions that had molded how she might interpret achievement and satisfaction. The excursion turned into a course of shedding the layers of molding, a stripping away of the veils that had hidden the real self.

In the organization of similar spirits who shared a comparable hunger for realness, Sarah found a local area that supported her expanding healthy identity. Discussions turned into an embroidery of shared weaknesses and aggregate development. The trading of thoughts and encounters made a ripe ground for contemplation, impelling every person towards a more profound comprehension of their real selves.

The excursion towards self-disclosure was not without its difficulties. Sarah experienced snapshots of uneasiness and opposition as she stood up to the shadows inside — the parts of herself that had for some time been consigned to the peripheries of awareness. However, with each step into the obscure, she found that the shadows held the keys to significant change.

The excursion turned into a dance of coordination — a fitting of the divided bits of self into a durable entirety. The shadows, once saw as foes, became partners during the time spent self-becoming. Sarah embraced the total of her being — the light and the dull, the qualities and the weaknesses — perceiving that credibility was not an objective but rather a continuous excursion.

In the cauldron of self-revelation, Sarah uncovered the force of weakness. She discovered that genuine strength lay not in apathetic obstruction but rather in the eagerness to be found completely, defects what not. The demonstration of opening up turned into a demonstration of boldness — an affirmation of the common mankind that bound people as they continued looking for legitimacy.

As the months unfurled, the groundbreaking excursion stretched out past the domains of the individual into the expert and cultural components of Sarah's life. The vocation, when a simple kind of revenue, turned into an expansion of her true self. She looked for arrangement between her expert interests and her qualities, imbuing reason into her undertakings.

The cultural stories of achievement and achievement went through investigation, and Sarah reclassified her measurements of satisfaction. It was as of now not tied in with adjusting to outer assumptions however about cutting a way that resounded with her bona fide goals. The quest for progress turned into a result of the arrangement among energy and reason.

The groundbreaking excursion additionally saturated Sarah's connections. The associations she produced were not generally founded on shallow assumptions or cultural standards. All things considered, they became vessels for shared development and understanding. Validness turned into the foundation of her associations, and she supported connections that praised the embodiment of every person.

The snapshot of significant self-revelation, which had been started by despondency, presently unfurled as a persistent story — an embroidery woven with the strings of versatility, credibility, and extraordinary development. Sarah, when restricted by the constraints of a biased personality, arose as a powerful power — a demonstration of the getting through limit of the human soul for reestablishment and self-completion.

As she remained at the slope of another section, Sarah conveyed with her the insight gathered from the excursion of self-revelation. The misfortune that had once appeared to be difficult had turned into an impetus for a transformation that rose above the limits of melancholy. The waterway of life, when changed by the flows of distress, presently streamed with reestablished force, cutting a way towards strange domains of plausibility.

The groundbreaking excursion was not set apart by a solitary revelation but rather by a nonstop course of development. Every day turned into a chance for self-reestablishment, an encouragement to investigate new aspects of personality. The excursion of self-disclosure, when moved by outer conditions, presently turned into a characteristic piece of Sarah's presence — a continuous journey towards a more true and satisfying life.

In the excellent embroidery of her story, the snapshot of significant self-revelation remained as a demonstration of the versatility of the human soul. It was an update that, even notwithstanding misfortune, people had an intrinsic limit with regards to development, variation, and the uncovering of their bona fide selves. The excursion, however testing, had turned into a festival of the complex dance among weakness and strength, shadows and light — a festival of the consistently unfurling venture towards self-becoming.

### 4.3 Internal and external conflicts reach a climax.

Inside the complex embroidery of Clara's life, a crescendo of interior and outer contentions had been consistently fabricating — an ensemble of strains that resounded through the passages of her cognizance and the outside scene of her reality. The struggles under the surface were the concealed fights pursued inside the openings of her psyche — a mind boggling dance between contending wants, fears, and goals.

The outside clashes, then again, appeared in the unmistakable world, entrapping Clara in a trap of conditions and connections that tried the constraints of her flexibility.

The primary types of dissension had exuded from the domain of Clara's struggles under the surface — a perplexing interchange of self-question, unfulfilled desires, and the unending quest for cultural assumptions. The reverberations of her internal conflict appeared in the endless addressing of her decisions and the biting insecurity that waited in the shadows of her viewpoints. Clara wrestled with the cacophony between the individual she sought to be and the individual she saw herself to be — an inner turmoil that turned into the pot for her excursion towards self-revelation.

As the unseen struggles heightened, outside pressures started to apply their impact on Clara's life. The requests of a high-stakes profession, the assumptions for familial commitments, and the complicated snare of relational connections became outer powers that pulled at the strings of her harmony. The outside clashes, similar to a tempest gathering not too far off, cast a shadow over the fragile equilibrium Clara had strived to keep up with.

The peak of inward and outside clashes joined in a snapshot of retribution — an essential crossroads that would characterize the direction of Clara's story. The impetus for this peak was a startling disclosure — an uncovering of bits of insight that had for some time been covered underneath the facade of cultural assumptions and individual deceptions. Clara faced the unmistakable real factors of her struggles under the surface, stripping away the layers of self-trickiness to uncover the crude and unvarnished bits of insight that lay underneath.

The inner turmoil, which had appeared as a battle among realness and similarity, arrived at its pinnacle. Clara, with a need to get going, left on an excursion of self-cross examination — a cycle that revealed the underlying drivers of her inside conflict. The cultural assumptions that had represented her decisions, the implicit feelings of trepidation that had controlled her desires, and the smothered voice of her valid self — all came to the front in a fountain of disclosure.

As Clara wrestled with the struggles under the surface, the outer contentions flooded with elevated force. The expert domain, when a wellspring of satisfaction, turned into a milestone where the conflict between private qualities and corporate assumptions worked out. The connections that had once given comfort presently stressed under the heaviness of implicit strains. Clara ended up exploring a maze of outer tensions, where the choices she made resonated through the interconnected trap of her expert and individual life.

The peak of contentions unfurled in a progression of vital minutes. Clara, done able to be held hostage by the deceptions of cultural assumptions, faced her bosses with a real to life affirmation of her actual longings and desires. The expert contentions, when stewing underneath the surface, emitted into a showdown that tried the limits of corporate standards.

Clara's genuineness, a power that had extended stayed lethargic, arose as an impetus for change — a specialist that tried to reshape the shapes of her expert presence.

The outside clashes stretched out past the limits of the working environment. Clara's own connections turned into a milestone where the conflict among independence and familial assumptions worked out. The implicit strains that had putrefied inside the elements of her family came to the front, making breaks that took steps to rethink the actual underpinnings of her emotionally supportive network.

The peak of struggles carried Clara eye to eye with decisions that rose above the polarity of good and bad. It was a snapshot of significant reflection — a point where Clara wrestled not just with the outside pressures that drag downward on her yet additionally with the struggles under the surface that had formed her reactions. The unwinding of the deceptions that had hidden her credible self turned into the key part for the choices she was going to make.

In the cauldron of contention, Clara went up against the feeling of dread toward disheartening others — an outer strain that had long held influence over her decisions. The peak turned into a statement of independence, as Clara decided to respect her credible self over the assumptions for other people. The unseen struggles, when a wellspring of self-question, presently turned into a repository of solidarity — a wellspring from which Clara attracted the boldness to stand firm despite outside pressures.

The outside clashes, however turbulent, turned into an impetus for Clara's own development. The conflicts in the expert domain moved her towards a redefinition of progress — one that lined up with her genuine goals as opposed to adjusting to predefined standards. The strains inside her family, however full of uneasiness, opened a space for legit discussions and a renegotiation of limits that regarded both independence and association.

As Clara explored the peak of contentions, she found an unforeseen partner inside the maze of affliction — flexibility. The contentions, instead of breaking her soul, turned into the pot that tempered her determination. Clara's process turned into a demonstration of the human limit with regards to development and change despite difficulty — an update that struggles, however testing, held the potential for significant transformation.

In the outcome of the peak, Clara remained at a junction — a place of difference where the ways of her inside and outer struggles converged. Her decisions at this time would decide the direction of her story. The contentions, as opposed to being difficult obstructions, became venturing stones towards a more credible and satisfying presence.

The unseen struggles, which had once been a wellspring of disagreement, presently turned into a wellspring of direction. Clara paid attention to the murmurs of her bona fide self, permitting the sense of direction of her qualities and yearnings to direct her decisions. The outer struggles, however still present, were at this point not abusive powers but instead difficulties that welcomed Clara to affirm her independence and rethink the forms of her connections and expert pursuits.

As Clara embraced the post-climactic period of her story, she perceived that clashes were not simple disturbances but rather open doors for development and self-revelation. The inside and outer tensions, when adversaries, became impetuses for the development of her personality. The peak, as opposed to being the zenith of a story, turned into a temporary point — an extension between the old and the new, among similarity and validness.

In the embroidery of Clara's life, the peak of contentions was not a decision but rather a preface to a continuous excursion of self-becoming. The struggles, inward and outer, became strings woven into the complicated story of her reality — an account that praised the strength of the human soul, the groundbreaking force of legitimacy, and the steady faith in the chance of rethinking one's way in the midst of the intricacies of life.

In the pot of life's wild process, Susan ended up remaining at the cliff of a climactic second — a convergence where inward and outer contentions combined, making a bedlam of difficulties that requested her consideration and strength. The contentions, both inside the profundities of her being and in the outer world that encompassed her, had been consistently constructing, winding around a perplexing embroidery of pressure and battle. Presently, as the crescendo arrived at its peak, Susan confronted a significant point that would characterize the direction of her story.

Inside, the contentions were well established in the perplexing scene of Susan's feelings, convictions, and yearnings. A feeling of unfulfillment and fretfulness had flourished, developing into a determined propensity of discontent that hued her view of self and reason. The unseen fits of turmoil were a fight between the individual she trusted herself to be and the individual she tried to become — a battle that stewed underneath the surface, looking for goal.

The reverberations of self-question resonated inside Susan's viewpoints, creating shaded areas over her certainty and obfuscating her feeling of personality. The unseen struggles appeared as a tireless addressing — an unending cross examination of her decisions, her value, and the realness of the existence she was driving. The climactic second was a challenge to face these inside storms head-on, to dive into the profundities of her spirit and disentangle the bunches of vulnerability that bound her.

Remotely, the struggles appeared in the unmistakable world that Susan explored — a world hued by connections, cultural assumptions, and the unusual touches of destiny.

The expert circle, when a wellspring of dependability, had turned into a war zone where the conflict between private qualities and corporate requests worked out. Susan ended up trapped in the complexities of work environment elements, where the quest for progress crashed into the limits of moral split the difference.

The outer contentions stretched out past the work environment, meshing into the texture of Susan's own connections. The assumptions for family, the requests of fellowships, and the cultural standards that recommended the shapes of an effective life made a snare of outer tensions that pulled at the edges of her harmony. The peak of struggles allured Susan to stand up to these outer powers, to explore the perplexing dance among independence and cultural assumptions.

The impetus for this climactic second came as a progression of occasions — a surprising spot of destiny that upset the sensitive equilibrium Susan had strived to keep up with. An expert difficulty, unanticipated changes in private connections, and a significant feeling of dissatisfaction combined to make a powerful coincidence of difficulties. The struggles, both inside and outside, mixed into a particular story pressure that requested goal.

In the cauldron of the climactic second, Susan confronted the overwhelming errand of reflection — an excursion into the maze of her unseen struggles. Oneself uncertainty that had waited in the shadows presently arose into the cruel light of mindfulness. The inquiries that had a distant memory unanswered requested lucidity, and Susan set out on a course of unwinding the layers of her personality.

The unseen fits of turmoil arrived at their peak as Susan faced the foundations of her discontent. The goals she had held onto, the fantasies that had assumed a lower priority, and the trade offs she had made for similarity — all arose as central focuses in her inner scene. The climactic second turned into a retribution with realness, a call to adjust her life to the most genuine articulations of her self.

As Susan explored the maze of unseen struggles, she found surprising supplies of solidarity and strength inside herself. The questions that had once deadened her became venturing stones towards self-revelation. The climactic second, as opposed to being a plunge into despair, turned into a climb into the domains of strengthening — an acknowledgment that the ability to shape her story lay inside her grip.

Remotely, the struggles unfurled in a progression of conflicts and decisions that would reclassify Susan's way. The expert circle turned into a landmark where moral contemplations conflicted with corporate assumptions. The peak of struggles requested Susan to pursue decisions that rose above the quick gains of expert achievement — a decision among respectability and congruity.

In the domain of individual connections, Susan confronted the test of defining limits and declaring her independence. The outside clashes arrived at a crescendo as she faced the assumptions for family and the cultural standards that had directed her way of living. The climactic second turned into a chance for Susan to reclassify the conditions of her connections, to convey her necessities and desires with a newly discovered lucidity.

As the outer contentions arrived at their peak, Susan wrestled with the feeling of dread toward frustrating others — a trepidation profoundly imbued in the cultural molding that had formed her decisions. The climactic second was a demonstration of her boldness, as she picked credibility over pacification, independence over congruity. The outer struggles, when impressive foes, became impetuses for the reshaping of her connections and the redefinition of her limits.

The repercussions of the climactic second denoted a time of contemplation and reconstructing for Susan. The unseen struggles, however not completely settled, had moved from a condition of strife to a more nuanced understanding. Susan embraced the continuous course of self-disclosure, perceiving that the excursion towards genuineness was not a direct way but rather a developing story.

Remotely, the struggles made a permanent imprint on Susan's expert and individual life. Her decisions in the climactic second resounded through the passages of her profession, making a gradually expanding influence that changed the elements of her work environment. In her own connections, the climactic decisions started a course of renegotiation and recalibration — an excursion towards connections grounded in shared understanding and regard.

The climactic second, as opposed to being an endpoint, turned into an intersection for Susan — a crossroads where the directions of her interior and outside clashes converged. The contentions, both inward and outside, became strings woven into the embroidery of her story. The climactic second, however testing, turned into an impetus for development, self-revelation, and the strengthening to shape her story based on her conditions.

As Susan pushed ahead, she conveyed with her the illustrations gathered from the climactic second. The struggles, once saw as hindrances, had become impetuses for change. The interior questions had given way to a newly discovered identity confirmation, and the outer tensions had become open doors for declaring validness and independence.

In the fantastic embroidery of Susan's life, the climactic second remained as a demonstration of the flexibility of the human soul. It was an update that contentions, however testing, held the potential for development and self-revelation. The story, a long way from being a straight movement, unfurled as a powerful interaction among inner and outer powers — a dance of flexibility, credibility, and the getting through plausibility of self-reevaluation.

# Chapter 5

### Revelation and Insight

In the immense spread of human life, the quest for information has been a getting through venture, set apart by snapshots of disclosure and knowledge that shape the course of civilizations. An excursion rises above reality, winding through the embroidery of mankind's set of experiences, interfacing unique strings of intelligence and understanding. Disclosure and knowledge, similar to twin points of support, stand at the center of this scholarly odyssey, directing humankind through the maze of its own reality.

Disclosure, in its substance, is the divulging of bits of insight concealed in the shadows of obliviousness. It is the unexpected enlightenment of the brain, a vast revealing that uncovered the covered parts of the real world. All through the chronicles of history, people and social orders have been slung into new domains of understanding through brilliant encounters that modify the texture of their insight. These minutes resemble lightning fasteners that penetrate the haziness, illuminating the beforehand inconspicuous features of the world.

The historical backdrop of strict practices is packed with records of significant disclosures that have changed the otherworldly scenes of whole civic establishments. From the consuming shrubbery of Moses to the cavern of Hira where the Quran was uncovered to Prophet Muhammad, these occurrences of heavenly correspondence have made a permanent imprint on the shared mindset of billions. The disclosure isn't restricted to the holy texts alone; it penetrates the domains of workmanship, science, and reasoning, igniting outlook changes that reclassify the limits of human comprehension.

In the domain of science, the divulging of the heliocentric model by Copernicus remains as a stupendous disclosure that broke the geocentric perspective. The universe, once accepted to spin around the Earth, was presently perceived as a perplexing dance of divine bodies represented by widespread regulations. Copernicus' disclosure set up for the logical transformation, making ready for masterminds like Galileo, Kepler, and Newton to additionally disentangle the secrets of the universe.

Essentially, in the realm of reasoning, the moral story of the cavern in Plato's "Republic" fills in as a strong figurative disclosure. The detainees, tied in a dim cavern, see just shadows on the wall, confusing them with the real world. The disclosure happens when one detainee is liberated, presented to the blinding light of the sun, and understands the real essence of the world past the cavern. This purposeful anecdote exemplifies the extraordinary force of disclosure, lifting the cloak of obliviousness to uncover the higher bits of insight that lie past shallow appearances.

In any case, disclosure isn't exclusively the area of the remarkable or the heavenly. It can likewise appear in the peaceful snapshots of reflection and self-disclosure. The unexpected acknowledgment of a significant individual truth, the "Aha!" second that proclaims a forward leap in one's comprehension, is a type of disclosure. These disclosures, however less self important in scale, are no less critical in molding the course of individual lives.

Knowledge, then again, is the consequence of a more profound, supported consideration and understanding. It is the result of a psyche took part in the many-sided dance of examination, union, and reflection. While disclosure might be the flash that lights the fire of understanding, knowledge is the consistent shine that exudes from a brain that looks to fathom the intricacies of the world.

In the logical domain, knowledge frequently emerges from the patient perception of normal peculiarities and the fastidious examination of information. Darwin's hypothesis of development, for example, didn't rise up out of a solitary life-changing second yet was the zenith of long periods of fastidious perception, assortment of examples, and thorough examination of natural variety. His knowledge into the components of normal choice changed science and our comprehension of life's perplexing web.

Also, the field of material science has been molded by the significant experiences of people like Albert Einstein. His hypothesis of relativity, conceived out of a profound thought of the idea of reality, changed how we might interpret the universe. Einstein's bits of knowledge were not the consequence of unexpected disclosure but rather of relentless scholarly request and an eagerness to scrutinize the groundworks of laid out insight.

In way of thinking, existentialist masterminds like Jean-Paul Sartre and Albert Camus dug into the human condition with significant knowledge. Their appearance on the idea of presence, opportunity, and the ridiculousness of life were not conceived out of heavenly disclosure but rather rose up out of a thorough assessment of the human experience. Knowledge, in this unique situation, is the result of philosophical request and the persistent quest for figuring out the intricacies of human life.

Writing, as well, is a domain where knowledge winds around its story strings. Crafted by authors like Fyodor Dostoevsky and Virginia Woolf dive into the profundities of the human mind, offering experiences into the complexities of human feelings and connections. These creators are not simple transports of stories but rather modelers of knowledge, developing accounts that resound with the all inclusive bits of insight of the human experience.

In the domain of brain science, crafted by pioneers like Sigmund Freud and Carl Jung is set apart by bits of knowledge into the operations of the human psyche. Freud's investigation of the oblivious and Jung's idea of the aggregate oblivious opened new roads for figuring out human way of behaving and the intricacies of the mind. Their bits of knowledge, established in the cautious assessment of individual and aggregate encounters, keep on impacting the area of brain research.

The transaction among disclosure and knowledge is clear during the time spent imaginative creation. Craftsmen, whether painters, performers, or scholars, frequently experience snapshots of disclosure that motivate their inventive undertakings. These disclosures might come as dreams, unexpected motivations, or a profound association with the dream. In any case, the groundbreaking force of craftsmanship lies in these life-changing minutes as well as in the craftsman's capacity to make an interpretation of that motivation into a work of getting through knowledge.

The works of art of Vincent van Gogh, for example, are implanted with the craftsman's significant experiences into the excellence and disturbance of presence. Van Gogh's "Brilliant Evening" isn't simply a portrayal of a night sky however a visual articulation of the craftsman's internal conflict and his impression of the vast powers at play. The disclosure of the brilliant night turns into a vehicle for conveying a more profound understanding into the human condition.

Melodic pieces, as well, frequently rise out of a combination of disclosure and understanding. The orchestras of Beethoven, the shows of Mozart, and the ad libs of jazz performers all bear the engraving of snapshots of disclosure that flash innovative articulation. However, it is the craftsman's knowledge into the construction, concordance, and profound reverberation of their specialty that lifts these works to the domain of ageless workmanship.

The connection among disclosure and understanding stretches out past the person to shape the elements of cultural advancement. Upheavals, whether political, social, or logical, frequently start with a disclosure that uncovered the treacheries or impediments of existing frameworks. The knowledge, then, at that point, lies in the aggregate comprehension of the requirement for change and the plan of a dream for a superior future.

The Modern Upset, for instance, was energized by the disclosure of new innovative conceivable outcomes, for example, steam power and motorized creation. In any case, the cultural change that resulted required the disclosure of these developments as well as the knowledge to saddle them to improve humankind. The molding of establishments, the plan of regulations, and the improvement of moral structures were results of aggregate understanding that went with the impactful snapshot of innovative headway.

In the domain of civil rights, disclosures of foundational disparities and treacheries have ignited developments for change. The Social liberties Development in the US, for example, was impelled by the disclosure of the unmistakable real factors of racial segregation. In any case, the enduring effect of the development relied upon the aggregate knowledge of pioneers and activists who imagined a general public based on standards of correspondence and equity.

The complicated dance among disclosure and knowledge isn't restricted to the domains of accomplishment and progress. It additionally unfurls notwithstanding difficulty and existential difficulties. The human reaction to emergencies frequently includes a course of disclosure, where people and social orders face the cruel real factors of their conditions. Whether as an individual emergency or a worldwide pandemic, these snapshots of disclosure force a reconsideration of needs and points of view.

The Coronavirus pandemic, for instance, uncovered the weaknesses and interconnectedness of worldwide frameworks. The disclosure of the delicacy of medical services, financial, and social designs incited an aggregate retribution with the requirement for flexibility and versatility. Notwithstanding, the experiences acquired from this disclosure will decide the direction of cultural reactions and the structure of additional powerful and fair frameworks in the post-pandemic world.

In the domain of self-awareness, the excursion towards self-disclosure frequently includes snapshots of disclosure that force people to face parts of themselves they might have disregarded or neglected.

Whether through thoughtfulness, treatment, or extraordinary educational encounters, these disclosures become impetuses for self-improvement. However, it is the continuous course of knowledge, the supported work to comprehend and coordinate these disclosures into one's life, that prompts enduring change.

The advantageous connection among disclosure and understanding stretches out into the texture of strict and otherworldly practices. Numerous magical encounters are outlined as snapshots of heavenly disclosure, where the limits between the limited and the endless haze. Whether through reflection, petition, or other pondering practices, people try to adjust themselves to these dramatic minutes, wanting to witness bits of insight past the cover of customary discernment.

Nonetheless, the spiritualist's process doesn't end with disclosure alone. The significant bits of knowledge acquired from these extraordinary encounters shape the's comprehension spiritualist might interpret the idea of presence, cognizance, and the heavenly. The spiritualist turns into a channel for bits of knowledge that, while established in the brilliant experience, reach out past the limits of individual cognizance to offer looks at general insights.

The union of disclosure and knowledge is additionally clear in the domain of training. The most common way of advancing frequently includes snapshots of disclosure when an idea snaps, and grasping sunrises on the student. Be that as it may, the development of genuine information requires more than disengaged disclosures. It requests the advancement of decisive reasoning, scientific abilities, and the capacity to apply bits of knowledge across assorted spaces.

The job of teachers, then, isn't only to work with snapshots of disclosure yet to direct understudies in the development of knowledge. It is the contrast between retaining realities and figuring out standards, between getting information and creating insight. The most groundbreaking instructive encounters are those that support both the life-changing flash of interest and the supported sparkle of quick comprehension.

In the domain of innovation and development, the unfurling account of disclosure and knowledge shapes the direction of progress. Mechanical forward leaps frequently rise up out of life-changing minutes, for example, the "aha!" revelations in research facilities or the abrupt experiences that lead to notable developments. Be that as it may, the capable and moral utilization of innovation requires progressing knowledge into its cultural effect, moral contemplations, and long haul outcomes.

The coming of man-made brainpower, for example, presents both dramatic conceivable outcomes and moral difficulties. The disclosure of machines outperforming human knowledge compels us to go up against existential inquiries regarding the idea of awareness and the moral ramifications of making conscious creatures.

The bits of knowledge acquired from these disclosures will decide the moral systems and administrative measures expected to explore the advancing scene of man-made intelligence.

The fragile harmony among disclosure and understanding is additionally clear in the domains of legislative issues and administration. Political insurgencies frequently start with a disclosure of foundational treacheries or maltreatments of force. In any case, the enduring effect of these unrests relies upon the bits of knowledge of political pioneers and social orders in making manageable frameworks of administration. The fragile dance between the life-changing push for change and the keen development of new political designs characterizes the course of countries.

With regards to natural stewardship, the disclosures of biological emergencies, environmental change, and biodiversity misfortune have incited a worldwide arousing to the dire requirement for maintainable practices. The experiences acquired from these disclosures go past simple attention to direct the definition of arrangements, worldwide collaboration, and individual way of life changes important to address the perplexing difficulties confronting the planet.

The human mission for disclosure and knowledge stretches out to the investigation of space. The disclosures presented by telescopes, space tests, and galactic perceptions have extended how we might interpret the universe. Be that as it may, the experiences acquired from these disclosures go past the simple gathering of information about far off systems. They motivate consideration about our position in the universe, the chance of extraterrestrial life, and the philosophical ramifications of vast investigation.

The fragile transaction among disclosure and understanding is definitely not a straight or unsurprising cycle. It is a unique dance, a musical stream that winds through the texture of human experience. It requires a receptiveness to the obscure, a readiness to address suppositions, and a promise to the continuous quest for understanding. Disclosure and understanding are not contradicting powers but rather integral components that, when fit, move the human soul towards steadily growing skylines of information.

As we explore the flows of disclosure and knowledge, we are called to embrace the double idea of this scholarly excursion. The life-changing minutes, whether terrific or unpretentious, act as reference points of motivation that stir the brain to additional opportunities. These minutes are the astronomical sparkles that light the flames of interest and impel us into unfamiliar domains of investigation.

However, the excursion doesn't end with disclosure alone. The supported quest for knowledge permits us to explore the territory enlightened by these dramatic glimmers. Knowledge is the lamp that guides us through the complexities of understanding, assisting us with knowing examples, associations, and more profound implications. The consistent fire endures in any event, when the underlying flash of disclosure has blurred into memory.

In the fabulous woven artwork of human scholarly history, disclosure and understanding are the twist and weft, the entwined strings that give profundity and wealth to the texture of information. They are not confined events but rather a persistent exchange, a dance that rises above the limits of existence. The disclosures of the past reverberation in the experiences of the present, and together, they make ready for the disclosures on the way.

In the hug of disclosure and understanding, humankind tracks down the compass to explore the tremendous ocean of information. It is an excursion set apart by snapshots of stunningness and marvel, minutes when the shroud is lifted, and the secrets of presence are exposed. An excursion requires the lowliness to recognize the constraints of our ongoing comprehension and the fortitude to wander into the domains of the unexplored world.

As we stand at the edge of a steadily extending skyline of disclosure, let us be aware of the sensitive dance among disclosure and understanding. Allow us to develop a feeling of scholarly interest that invites the disclosures that coax us forward. Allow us additionally to sustain the discipline of clever request that permits us to plumb the profundities of understanding.

In the combination of disclosure and knowledge, we track down not just the keys to opening the secrets of the universe yet additionally the insight to explore the intricacies of the human experience. It is an excursion without a last objective, a ceaseless mission that moves us forward into the domains of probability. In the terrific embroidery of disclosure and knowledge, we find the unfurling story of the human mind — a story that keeps on being composed with each new disclosure and each shrewd step into the unexplored world.

## 5.1 The protagonist gains a deeper understanding of themselves and the purpose of the journey.

In the immense embroidery of narrating, the hero's process is in many cases a significant investigation of self-disclosure and reason. As the story unfurls, the focal person sets out on a groundbreaking odyssey that rises above the outside challenges they face. It turns into an excursion into the profundities of their own mind, a journey for significance and grasping that reflects the all inclusive human experience.

At the start, the hero might be driven by outer objectives — a mission for treasure, the quest for equity, or the longing for reclamation. These outer targets act as impetuses, pushing the person into the obscure and making way for a progression of experiences, preliminaries, and disclosures. However, as the excursion advances, the genuine meaning of the mission frequently uncovers itself not in the outer triumphs or losses but rather in the inner changes that happen inside the hero.

The course of self-disclosure is in many cases steady, set apart by snapshots of contemplation and disclosure. The hero, confronting difficulties that test their strength and character, starts to stand up to more profound layers of their own personality. It might include returning to past injuries, defying unsettled clashes, or addressing long-held convictions. This inward excursion is pretty much as misleading and erratic as the outer difficulties the hero countenances, and it requires a mental fortitude that stretches out past actual ability.

One part of the hero's self-revelation is the affirmation of weaknesses and flaws. In the underlying phases of the excursion, the person might extend a picture of power or apathy, covering the injuries that lie underneath the surface. Nonetheless, as the account unfurls, the hero is constrained to defy these weaknesses. It is in snapshots of emergency and misery that the exterior disintegrates, uncovering the genuine, imperfect human underneath.

This disclosure of weakness is definitely not an indication of shortcoming yet a demonstration of the genuineness of the hero's excursion. It adapts the person, cultivating compassion and appeal with the crowd. The crowd, thus, sees impressions of their own battles and weaknesses reflected in the hero's insight, producing a more profound close to home association with the story.

As the hero wrestles with their weaknesses, they frequently experience tutors or partners who assume a critical part in directing them on their excursion of self-revelation. These guides might be shrewd sages, experienced voyagers, or even impossible partners whose own accounts reflect the hero's conflicts under the surface. Through the tutor's direction, the hero acquires experiences into their own mind, faces inward evil presences, and learns important examples about strength and self-acknowledgment.

The guide's job isn't simply to give shrewdness however to act as a mirror, reflecting back to the hero parts of themselves that might have been disregarded or denied. This intelligent capability catalyzes the hero's contemplative process, provoking them to address suspicions, challenge previously established inclinations, and reexamine their own inspirations. Along these lines, the coach turns into an impetus for the hero's more profound comprehension of their own character and reason.

The excursion of self-disclosure is frequently entwined with the hero's investigation of their own qualities and convictions. As they explore the difficulties of the outer world, they are compelled to defy moral issues, moral binds, and the outcomes of their decisions. These snapshots of moral retribution become critical points in the hero's inward excursion, forming their developing identity and reason.

The unseen struggles emerging from moral situations add to the lavishness and intricacy of the hero's personality. The battle among good and bad, dependability and disloyalty, obligation and individual craving, turns into a pot for self-assessment.

It is through these moral difficulties that the hero acquires bits of knowledge into the subtleties of their own ethical compass, prompting a more profound comprehension of the rules that guide their activities.

The excursion of self-revelation is certainly not a straight movement however a repetitive course of development and relapse. The hero might encounter breakthrough moments and disclosure, just to be dove once more into snapshots of uncertainty and disarray. This rhythmic movement make a powerful inside scene, reflecting the capriciousness of life's excursion. The hero's capacity to explore these patterns of self-revelation mirrors their flexibility and limit with respect to development.

Necessary to the hero's interior process is the investigation of their own apprehensions and uncertainties. Similarly as the outside excursion might include confronting legendary beasts or considerable foes, the interior excursion requires the hero to stand up to the beasts inside — their own feelings of trepidation, questions, and unsettled injuries. This conflict is in many cases more overwhelming than any outside enemy, requiring the hero to dig into the most obscure openings of their own mind.

The goal of these unseen fits of turmoil isn't tied in with killing feelings of dread yet about embracing them, figuring out their starting points, and rising above their deadening hold. It is a course of self-acknowledgment and joining, where the hero figures out how to channel dread into boldness and change weakness into strength. This inside speculative chemistry is a urgent part of the hero's excursion, denoting a huge achievement as they continued looking for self-disclosure.

The hero's developing comprehension of themselves is unpredictably attached to the unfurling disclosures about the reason for their excursion. What might have at first appeared to be a direct mission for outside accomplishment — a lost relic, the loss of a reprobate — changes into a more significant investigation of the hero's inward scene. The outside targets act as a figurative framework whereupon the more deeply layers of the inner excursion are built.

The motivation behind the excursion, thusly, rises above the material or outer objectives. It turns into a journey for importance, character, and a feeling of one's spot in the fantastic embroidery of presence. This change in context reexamines the account, lifting it from a simple experience story to a philosophical investigation of the human condition.

As the hero acquires experiences into their own inspirations and stands up to the existential inquiries that support their excursion, they become sensitive to a higher reason. This reason might be subtle and conceptual, established in topics of affection, equity, reclamation, or amazing quality. A reason rises above the prompt targets of the journey and lines up with general subjects that resound across societies and ages.

The hero's more profound comprehension of themselves and the reason for the excursion frequently finishes in a snapshot of significant disclosure. This disclosure is certainly not a simple unexpected development or an abrupt development however a climactic acknowledgment that blends the inward and outside components of the story. It is an epiphany where the hero, having explored the maze of their own mind, sees the interconnected strings that weave the texture of their reality.

This impactful second is groundbreaking, denoting the hero's transformation into an additional illuminated and mindful person. It is a snapshot of significant coordination, where the divided bits of the hero's character blend into an additional bound together and genuine entirety. The reason for the excursion, presently completely got it, turns into a directing light that enlightens the way ahead.

The hero's recently discovered understanding isn't without its difficulties. The disclosures might carry with them a significant weight of liability or an increased consciousness of the intricacies of presence. The hero might wrestle with the heaviness of their own decisions, the outcomes of their activities, and the acknowledgment that the excursion of self-revelation is a continuous interaction instead of an objective.

In the outcome of the life-changing second, the hero might go through a time of reflection and solidification. This stage permits them to incorporate the bits of knowledge acquired, accommodate with the illustrations learned, and get ready for the last phases of the outer mission. The inward and outer components of the account join, making way for the hero's definitive showdown with the difficulties that started their excursion.

The blend of self-revelation and the motivation behind the excursion is many times reflected in the outside goal of the story. The hero, outfitted with a more profound comprehension of themselves and an explained feeling of direction, faces the peak of their outside mission. This conflict might include an impressive foe, a definitive decision, or an emblematic demonstration that implies the perfection of the hero's development.

The outside goal isn't simply a victory over outer enemies yet an impression of the hero's inside triumph. The fights battled inside the openings of the hero's mind track down their outside appearance in the climactic occasions that carry the story to its peak. The goal turns into an illustration for the hero's coordination of their inward and external universes.

The repercussions of the outer goal isn't really a clean decision or a slick tying of remaining details. All things considered, it could be an impression of the continuous idea of the hero's excursion. Life, similar to the story, is a consistent pattern of difficulties and development, and the hero's process fills in as a microcosm of this timeless cycle.

The goal turns into a venturing stone, not an endpoint, as the hero proceeds to develop and confront new skylines.The excursion of self-revelation, entwined with the motivation behind the journey, makes a permanent imprint on the hero's personality.

**5.2 Unveiling of hidden truths and mysteries.**

In the domains of narrating, there exists an enduring interest with the uncovering of stowed away insights and secrets. Whether through the pages of a novel, the edges of a film, or the story bends of old fantasies, the investigation of covered real factors enthralls the human creative mind. The story venture, frequently impelled by the journey for understanding, leaves on a mission to strip back the layers of mystery, uncovering bits of insight that lay covered in the shroud of lack of clarity.

The charm of stowed away bits of insight lies in their capability to reshape discernments, challenge suppositions, and flash disclosures that rise above the common. A topical propensity rises above kinds and ages, clearing a path through the texture of human narrating. From the baffling pyramids of Egypt to the surreptitious social orders of paranoid ideas, the human account is overflowing with stories of the quest for buried information.

At the core of these stories is in many cases a hero — a courageous searcher, an inquisitive brain, or an accidental legend — brought into the gravitational draw of the unexplored world. The excursion to reveal stowed away insights turns into a story support, controlling the hero through a maze of difficulties, puzzles, and mysterious experiences. The unfurling of these secrets isn't simply a plot gadget yet a topical investigation that reflects the human journey for understanding and illumination.

The uncovering of stowed away bits of insight isn't restricted to the fantastical domains of fiction. History itself is an embroidery woven with the strings of disclosures, revelations, and the tenacious quest for information. Logical forward leaps, archeological discoveries, and authentic disclosures are indications of humankind's lasting drive to disentangle the secrets that shroud the past, present, and future.

In the artistic area, the theme of stowed away insights frequently appears as antiquated texts, secretive images, or failed to remember legend. These antiques act as keys, opening ways to domains of information that have long escaped human cognizance. From the Necronomicon of H.P. Lovecraft to the looks of Umberto Eco's "The Name of the Rose," writing winds around stories that raise the journey for buried insights to a vast and mystical scale.

The disentangling of these artistic secrets frequently rises above the limits of the actual world, diving into the domains of the extraordinary and the obscure. Mysterious customs, enchanted ancient rarities, and the interaction of light and shadow become account apparatuses that guide

characters and perusers the same through the overly complex passages of stowed away information. It is a dance among disclosure and disguise, with every disclosure opening new entryways into the unexplored world.

The idea of stowed away bits of insight expands its ringlets into the class of secret and criminal investigator fiction, where the revealing of mysteries is certainly not an infinite disclosure yet a fastidious disentangling of signs and proof. From Arthur Conan Doyle's Sherlock Holmes to Agatha Christie's Hercule Poirot, fictitious investigators act as courses for the human craving to uncover stowed away insights and carry equity to the darkened.

In the realistic domain, the disclosing of stowed away insights is much of the time joined by climatic visuals, tormenting music, and the sensational pacing of an all around created spine chiller. From the chiaroscuro-lit roads of film noir to the supernatural scenes of sci-fi, movie producers tackle the force of visual narrating to drench crowds in stories that depend on the disclosure of hidden real factors.

Paranoid notions, a type no matter what anyone else might think, blossom with the disclosing of stowed away bits of insight that purportedly lie underneath the outer layer of true stories. These accounts frequently investigate the shadowy domains of government smoke screens, extraterrestrial experiences, and mystery social orders making things happen from the shadows. While numerous paranoid fears might need experimental proof, they feature a social interest with the possibility that strong powers are organizing occasions in the background, stowed away from general visibility.

The representative domain of folklore is packed with stories based on the quest for buried bits of insight. In the Greek legend of Orpheus and Eurydice, Orpheus plunges into the hidden world to safeguard his darling, divulging the secrets of life and demise. Essentially, the mission for the Sacred goal in Arthurian legends is an emblematic excursion that entwines the profound and the natural, with knights setting out on a journey to uncover the heavenly secrets.

Strict texts, as well, are loaded down with stories of disclosure and the uncovering of heavenly bits of insight. The scriptural story of Moses getting the Ten Decrees on Mount Sinai is a significant snapshot of heavenly divulgence, an enormous revealing that shapes the moral underpinnings of monotheistic religions. The Quran, the sacred book of Islam, is viewed as a disclosure to the Prophet Muhammad, uncovering the expressions of God to direct humankind.

The disclosing of stowed away bits of insight isn't exclusively a topical investigation in fiction; it is a lived insight in the logical quest for information. The logical technique itself is a deliberate way to deal with divulging the secret functions of the regular world. Through perception, trial and error, and investigation, researchers endeavor to uncover the fundamental insights overseeing the universe, from the tiny domains of quantum material science to the huge breadths of the universe.

The historical backdrop of science is accentuated by snapshots of outlook changing disclosures — Copernicus' heliocentric model, Darwin's hypothesis of advancement, Einstein's hypothesis of relativity — all of which uncovered secret insights about the idea of the universe. The logical journey for information is a demonstration of the human ability to penetrate the cloak of obliviousness and uncover the basic rules that oversee the world.

The revealing of stowed away bits of insight isn't generally a clear excursion. It is loaded with difficulties, obstruction, and the agitating acknowledgment that a few secrets might remain perpetually outside the ability to understand of human comprehension. The figurative excursion of divulging isn't generally a victory; it might likewise be a plunge into the chasm of the obscure, where the searcher wrestles with the restrictions of human cognizance and the existential inquiries that lie at the core of the human experience.

The subject of stowed away insights additionally tracks down reverberation in the domain of brain science and self-disclosure. The human mind, similar to an old maze, harbors layers of oblivious contemplations, recollections, and wants ready to be revealed. Therapy, spearheaded by Sigmund Freud and later extended via Carl Jung, is a restorative excursion that looks to uncover the secret insights of the mind, exposing subdued feelings and unsettled clashes.

The figurative uncovering of stowed away insights isn't generally a singular undertaking. It frequently includes relational elements, where connections and associations become necessary to the disclosure cycle. The divulging might be a common excursion, with characters, partners, or networks teaming up to translate enigmatic codes, unravel old predictions, or uncover stowed away schemes. These stories highlight the common part of the human journey for understanding and the common obligation of divulging bits of insight that influence the system.

The excursion to reveal stowed away bits of insight isn't restricted to outside scenes or scholarly pursuits; it additionally unfurls inside the inward openings of the human heart. The mission for self-revelation, character, and genuineness is a story string woven into innumerable stories. Characters wrestle with their own secret bits of insight, facing individual devils, and looking to figure out the intricacies of their own inspirations and wants.

The divulging of stowed away insights, whether outside or inside, is frequently joined by snapshots of disclosure — revelations, moments of realization, and unexpected experiences that enlighten the dimness of obliviousness. These life-changing minutes might come as a blaze of motivation, a fantasy, or a significant experience that modifies the direction of the story. They act as account crescendos, checking critical focuses in the hero's excursion and impelling the story forward.

In the scholarly method of foretelling, creators drop unobtrusive clues and signs that portend future disclosures, making a feeling of expectation and strain. The disclosing of stowed away insights is in many cases a painstakingly coordinated story dance, where the writer directs the peruser through a maze of conceivable outcomes, passing on breadcrumbs that lead to the possible disclosure. This story procedure draws in the peruser's creative mind, welcoming them to take part in the disentangling of secrets.

The disclosing of stowed away bits of insight is definitely not a solid subject however a complex investigation that envelops a range of classifications, tones, and story styles. It very well may be the main thrust in a high-stakes spine chiller, a scrutinizing venture in philosophical fiction, a grandiose disclosure in sci-fi, or a mysterious investigation in dream. The subject adjusts to the shapes of the account, offering narrators a flexible material on which to paint stories of disclosure, disclosure, and the never-ending mission for understanding.

### 5.3 Integration of newfound wisdom to navigate the path ahead.

In the fabulous embroidery of human life, the excursion of self-disclosure frequently prompts the procurement of recently discovered shrewdness — a repository of bits of knowledge and understanding that rises out of the pot of encounters, difficulties, and snapshots of disclosure. This supply of insight, a long way from being a static assortment of information, turns into a unique power that shapes the singular's discernment, choices, and activities. The reconciliation of this freshly discovered shrewdness is a groundbreaking cycle, a combination that permits the person to explore the way forward with an elevated feeling of direction, flexibility, and edification.

The excursion of self-revelation, set apart by its exciting bends in the road, uncovers aspects of the person that were recently clouded. A cycle reaches out past the shallow layers of character, digging into the profundities of individual qualities, convictions, and inspirations. The disclosures that rise out of this excursion frequently act as the structure blocks of intelligence — a blend of mindfulness, compassion, and a nuanced comprehension of the intricacies of life.

Shrewdness, in its embodiment, isn't simply the gathering of realities or the dominance of a specific expertise; rather, it is the capacity to recognize significance, make good decisions, and explore the complexities of human connections. The joining of freshly discovered intelligence is a comprehensive undertaking that requires a blend of scholarly, profound, and moral aspects. It's anything but a direct interaction yet a nonstop development, an excursion without a proper objective where every disclosure adds to the mosaic of shrewdness.

The coordination of freshly discovered insight frequently starts with a course of reflection — a contemplative assessment of the illustrations took in, the difficulties confronted, and the extraordinary minutes experienced en route. This intelligent delay permits the person to distil the quintessence of their encounters, separating the center standards and experiences that will shape the bedrock of their advancing insight.

The joining system is likewise significantly impacted by the connections and associations manufactured during the excursion of self-disclosure. Connections with guides, partners, and even foes add to the's comprehension singular might interpret themselves and the world. Shrewdness, frequently gathered from the common thinking of others, turns into a cooperative endeavor, an intertwining of different points of view that enhance the embroidery of the person's own bits of knowledge.

Coaches, specifically, assume a vital part in the mix of newly discovered shrewdness. Their direction, tempered by experience and prepared with a more profound comprehension of life's intricacies, turns into a reference point for the searcher exploring unknown waters. The coach gives information as well as a structure for wisdom, moral contemplations, and a compass for moral route. The mix of the coach's insight turns into a rudder that guides the person through the tempestuous oceans of independent direction.

The coordination of freshly discovered astuteness is likewise complicatedly associated with the development of the ability to understand people on a deeper level. The excursion of self-disclosure frequently carries the singular eye to eye with a range of feelings — bliss, distress, love, dread, and in the middle between. Insight involves not just the capacity to appreciate these feelings inside oneself yet in addition to identify with the close to home scenes of others.

The ability to understand people on a deeper level includes the ability to control one's own feelings, recognize the feelings of others, and explore relational associations with responsiveness and compassion. As newly discovered intelligence flourishes, it cultivates close to home strength — the capacity to endure the tempests of existence without neglecting to focus on one's basic beliefs and standards. This close to home versatility turns into a fundamental part of the person's navigational tool compartment, empowering them to climate affliction and arise with newly discovered strength and understanding.

The joining of newly discovered intelligence is definitely not a singular undertaking however a common and cultural cycle. The individual, formed by their one of a kind excursion, turns into a contributing part to the aggregate insight of humankind. This common thinking, drawn from different encounters and viewpoints, is a demonstration of the interconnected idea of human life. The individual, furnished with their coordinated insight, turns into a reference point that enlightens the way for other people, cultivating an aggregate excursion of development and edification.

In the domains of writing and folklore, the combination of newly discovered shrewdness frequently appears as the legend's excursion — an original story design where the hero goes through a groundbreaking cycle, secures shrewdness, and gets back to society with an aid for everyone's benefit.

From the old Greek legend Odysseus to the abstract wizards of J.K. Rowling's "Harry Potter" series, the legend's process reflects the general human experience of self-revelation and the coordination of insight.

One of the signs of incorporated astuteness is its application to independent direction. The individual, furnished with a more profound comprehension of themselves and the world, explores the intricacies of decisions with an insightful eye. Shrewdness impacts the dynamic cycle, guiding the individual away from impulsivity and momentary satisfaction toward decisions lined up with long haul prosperity and satisfaction.

The joining of recently discovered astuteness is especially apparent despite moral and moral predicaments. Insight gives an ethical compass, directing the person through the nuanced territory of good and bad. The choices made affected by incorporated intelligence are frequently intelligent of a higher moral structure, a pledge to rules that rise above quick gains or misfortunes.

In the midst of difficulty, the coordinated insight turns into a wellspring of versatility and backbone. The singular draws upon the illustrations took in, the ability to appreciate people on a profound level developed, and the moral standards embraced during the excursion of self-disclosure. This supply of incorporated shrewdness fills in as a wellspring of solidarity, enabling the person to explore difficulties with effortlessness, poise, and an undaunted obligation to their qualities.

The joining of newly discovered shrewdness likewise appears in the development of a development outlook — a conviction that difficulties and misfortunes are potential open doors for learning and development as opposed to unfavorable hindrances. This attitude, established in the comprehension that knowledge and capacities can be created through commitment and difficult work, lines up with the quintessence of astuteness. It encourages a versatility that embraces difficulties as venturing stones to additional comprehension and dominance.

The reconciliation interaction isn't without its difficulties. It requires an eagerness to stand up to awkward bits of insight, question profoundly instilled convictions, and recognize one's own frailty. The excursion of self-disclosure, with its disclosures and experiences, may uncover parts of the self that are challenging to accommodate. The combination of freshly discovered intelligence requests a gutsy showdown with these viewpoints, encouraging a healthy identity acknowledgment and credibility.

The mix of astuteness is additionally a continuous interaction, intelligent of the nonstop development of the person. Life unfurls in unusual ways, introducing new difficulties, open doors, and snapshots of disclosure.

Coordinated shrewdness embraces the ease of life, adjusting to changing conditions while residual moored in center standards. It is a dance among solidness and versatility, a powerful harmony that supports the person through the back and forth movement of presence.

With regards to initiative, the reconciliation of freshly discovered intelligence is a sign of powerful and visionary pioneers. Pioneers who encapsulate astuteness are not just talented chiefs but rather humane and far-located people who think about the more extensive ramifications of their activities. They move trust, cultivate cooperation, and explore hierarchical difficulties with an insightful and moral methodology.

The coordination of freshly discovered shrewdness likewise adds to a feeling of direction and significance throughout everyday life. Insight, got from a more profound comprehension of oneself and the world, adjusts the person to a feeling of direction that rises above material pursuits. This reason turns into a directing star, enlightening the way forward and injecting existence with a significant feeling of satisfaction and importance.

In the domain of relational connections, the combination of shrewdness significantly impacts the nature of associations. Shrewd people, receptive to their own feelings and compassionate to the encounters of others, explore associations with beauty and understanding. The incorporated insight turns into a scaffold that encourages further associations, settle clashes with poise, and develops a feeling of shared development and common help.

The reconciliation of recently discovered intelligence isn't an honor saved for the experienced or the matured. It is a likely innate in the human experience, open to people at different phases of life. The youthful, in their investigations and goals, can develop shrewdness as they explore the intricacies of character and reason. The combination of shrewdness is a long lasting excursion, unfurling in exceptional ways for every person.

The story of coordinating newly discovered insight isn't restricted to the individual; it stretches out to the cultural and worldwide levels. Social orders, similar to people, wrestle with aggregate difficulties, moral problems, and open doors for development. The coordinated insight of a general public is reflected in its social qualities, moral standards, and the capacity to adjust to changing conditions while saving basic beliefs.

Worldwide difficulties, for example, environmental change, social imbalance, and international strains, request a coordinated methodology established in aggregate insight. The interconnectedness of the world requires a cooperative exertion that rises above public boundaries and social contrasts. The incorporation of insight on a worldwide scale.

# Chapter 6

### The Road Less Traveled

The less common direction is much of the time the one that prompts revelation, development, and self-acknowledgment. A way separates from the very much trampled courses, enticing those ready to embrace the obscure and confront the difficulties that lie ahead. This figurative street is an image of distinction, strength, and the quest for one's extraordinary excursion through life.

Life is an excursion loaded up with decisions, and the less common direction addresses the decision to stray from the traditional and produce a particular way. This decision isn't without its challenges, as the more uncommon street is frequently full of vulnerability and deterrents. Nonetheless, definitively these difficulties can prompt significant self-awareness and a more profound comprehension of oneself.

Setting out on the less common direction requires mental fortitude and an eagerness to step outside one's usual range of familiarity. It requests a takeoff from the recognizable and an endeavor into the strange domain of one's true capacity. This excursion isn't for weak willed, yet for the people not entirely settled to investigate the wealth of life past the generally accepted way to go.

One of the critical parts of the less common direction is the component of decision. Life gives us a horde of ways, each driving somewhere new. The less common direction is certainly not a foreordained course yet a cognizant choice to take a course less visited by others. This decision is a demonstration of independence, a statement that one isn't content to just follow the group however is rather determined by a longing for something more significant and genuine.

As people explore the less common direction, they frequently experience difficulties and snags that test their determination. These difficulties are a necessary piece of the excursion, filling in as any open doors for development and self-revelation. Difficulty has an approach to uncovering one's actual person and versatility, forming people into more grounded, more competent renditions of themselves.

The less common direction isn't an easy route or a simple way; an excursion requires persistence and an eagerness to get through hardships. It might include overcoming fears, facing vulnerabilities, and exploring through new territory. However, definitively these difficulties make the excursion beneficial, as they add to the improvement of shrewdness, strength, and a more profound comprehension of life.

Besides, the less common direction is much of the time portrayed by a feeling of isolation. Not at all like very much trampled ways where many travel together, the more uncommon street might be a singular one. This isolation, nonetheless, isn't dejection but instead a chance for contemplation and self-reflection. It permits people to interface with their deepest considerations and sentiments, cultivating a more profound comprehension of their own cravings, values, and yearnings.

The less common direction is certainly not a one-size-fits-all excursion; it is an interesting and individual experience for every person who decides to set out on it. There is no recommended objective or timetable, and the actual excursion turns into a wellspring of significance and satisfaction. Each step taken on this street is a cognizant decision to embrace one's singularity and to really live.

As people progress along the less common direction, they might find that it prompts startling spots and unexpected open doors. The excursion turns into a dynamic and developing interaction, with exciting bends in the road that challenge assumptions and open up additional opportunities. Embracing the vulnerability of the less common direction is a fundamental part of the experience, as it considers the fortunate revelation of unexpected, yet invaluable treasures en route.

The less common direction is likewise an illustration for development and imagination. Frequently the trend-setters and imaginative masterminds decide to veer off from the ordinary and investigate a strange area.

These people will face challenges, rock the boat, and imagine potential outcomes past the restrictions of ordinary reasoning. In doing as such, they add to the progression of society and the extension of human information and understanding.

In the domain of connections, the less common direction can appear as the decision to seek after real associations and significant bonds. It might include the mental fortitude to communicate weakness, to convey transparently, and to encourage profound and genuine associations with others. Picking the less common direction in connections frequently requires breaking liberated from cultural assumptions and embracing a more veritable and purposeful way to deal with human association.

Besides, the less common direction is a call to realness. It urges people to be consistent with themselves, to embrace their uniqueness, and to live in arrangement with their qualities. In a world that frequently compels people to adjust and squeeze into predefined molds, picking realness turns into a progressive demonstration. A statement one's actual self is more important than cultural endorsement, and that the way to satisfaction lies in living really.

The less common direction isn't a dismissal of show for disobedience; rather, it is a purposeful decision to carry on with a day to day existence that is consistent with one's bona fide self. It is a dismissal of congruity for similarity and an acknowledgment that genuine satisfaction comes from living in arrangement with one's qualities, interests, and reason.

As people venture to every part of the less common direction, they might wind up addressing cultural standards and social assumptions. This scrutinizing isn't a dismissal of custom for defiance yet a smart assessment of whether these standards line up with one's qualities and goals. The less common direction welcomes people to basically survey cultural assumptions and to pick a way that resounds with their own inward compass.

The less common direction is a demonstration of the human soul's ability for strength and development. It recognizes that life is an excursion of ceaseless learning and self-revelation, and that the difficulties experienced en route are open doors for improvement. In confronting difficulty, people on the less common direction develop internal strength, versatility, and their very own significant comprehension abilities.

Moreover, the less common direction is a festival of variety and independence. It perceives that every individual's process is interesting and that there is nobody size-fits-all equation for a satisfying life. The variety of ways taken by people adds to the extravagance and intricacy of the human experience, making a mosaic of exceptional stories and points of view that enhance the structure holding the system together.

Picking the less common direction requires a takeoff from the traditional assumptions for progress. It challenges the idea that achievement is exclusively characterized by outside markers like riches, status, or cultural endorsement. All things considered, accomplishment on the less common direction is estimated by the level of arrangement between one's life and values, the profundity of significant associations, and the satisfaction got from living really.

The less common direction isn't without its snapshots of uncertainty and vulnerability. As people explore unfamiliar territory, they might scrutinize their decisions and wrestle with the feeling of dread toward the unexplored world. These snapshots of uncertainty, in any case, are an innate piece of the excursion, filling in as any open doors for thoughtfulness and reaffirmation of one's obligation to the picked way.

Notwithstanding question, the less common direction welcomes people to trust their instinct and internal insight. It energizes a more profound association with one's deepest cravings and desires, directing people toward a more genuine and satisfying life. Confiding in the excursion, even in snapshots of vulnerability, is a pivotal part of embracing the less common direction.

The less common direction isn't an objective however a consistent excursion of self-revelation and development. It is a guarantee to long lasting learning, an acknowledgment that there is something else to investigate, find, and comprehend.

The actual excursion turns into a wellspring of importance, as people take part in a continuous course of self-development and change.

As people progress along the less common direction, they might find that their points of view and needs develop. What once appeared to be significant may could not hope to compare to more profound, more significant pursuits. The less common direction welcomes people to rethink their qualities, needs, and objectives, guaranteeing that they line up with their valid selves and add to a feeling of direction and satisfaction.

Besides, the less common direction is an excursion of care and presence. It urges people to enjoy the lavishness of every second, to be completely present in their encounters, and to develop a profound appreciation for the magnificence of life. In a world portrayed by steady hecticness and interruption, the less common direction turns into a safe-haven for careful living and purposeful presence.

The less common direction is likewise a call to strength notwithstanding mishaps and disappointments. It recognizes that the excursion isn't generally smooth, and that people might experience hindrances and difficulties en route. Strength turns into a fundamental friend on the less common direction, permitting people to return quickly from misfortune, gain from disappointments, and proceed with the excursion with reestablished assurance.

Picking the less common direction is a demonstration of strengthening. It is a statement that one has the organization to shape their own predetermination and the boldness to manufacture a way that lines up with their bona fide self. In a world that frequently stresses outer approval and similarity, the less common direction turns into an image of individual strengthening and self-assurance.

The less common direction isn't a dismissal of local area or shared encounters. In actuality, it can prompt the arrangement of valid associations with similar people who share comparable qualities and yearnings. The excursion turns into a public encounter, as people.

### 6.1 The journey takes unexpected turns, leading to unexplored territories.

Life is a flighty excursion, set apart by exciting bends in the road that frequently take us to neglected domains. The illustration of an excursion is a strong one, exemplifying the quintessence of human life as a consistent movement through time and experience. As we explore the mind boggling pathways of life, we unavoidably experience surprising diversions that challenge our insights, test our flexibility, and lead us to new and unfamiliar scenes.

The excursion is an all inclusive representation, rising above social, geological, and transient limits. It typifies the sum of the human experience, from the snapshot of birth to the inescapable entry into the unexplored world. Each individual leaves on their exceptional excursion, formed by private decisions, outer conditions, and the exchange of different variables that impact the direction of life.

One of the main traits of the excursion is its eccentricism. Similar as an unfamiliar guide, life unfurls in manners that can't be totally expected or controlled.

Surprising turns introduce themselves, changing the direction we had imagined and testing our versatility. It is in these unexpected turns that the genuine embodiment of the excursion is uncovered, expecting us to explore through vagueness and vulnerability.

The neglected domains of life address open doors for development, learning, and self-revelation. Whenever confronted with surprising difficulties or open doors, people are constrained to take advantage of their internal assets, drawing upon strength, imagination, and versatility to manufacture a way ahead. It is in these unfamiliar domains that we frequently track down secret possibilities, torpid abilities, and undiscovered supplies of solidarity.

The excursion's surprising turns might appear in different structures — profession changes, individual connections, wellbeing challenges, or unexpected open doors. Each diversion presents an extraordinary situation, requesting a reaction that is both smart and versatile. How people explore these snapshots of vulnerability can shape the course of their excursion and impact the individual they become.

Besides, the excursion is certainly not a single undertaking; it is unpredictably woven with the strings of human associations. Connections structure a huge piece of the landscape, impacting the idea of the excursion and giving friendship en route. Collaborations with others present new viewpoints, expand skylines, and add to the extravagance of the general insight.

As the excursion unfurls, people frequently wind up at intersection, confronted with choices that can possibly adjust their way of living. These choice focuses are basic crossroads, where decisions are made, and ways are chosen. The results of these choices resonate through the excursion, forming future encounters and impacting the unfurling account.

It is despite vulnerability that self-improvement frequently blooms. The difficulties presented by neglected regions test people's cutoff points, inciting them to address suppositions, adjust to new conditions, and develop versatility. Difficulty turns into an impetus for self-disclosure, uncovering qualities that might have stayed torpid without any difficulties.

The excursion's surprising turns additionally offer an encouragement to embrace change. Change, whether expected or unexpected, is an intrinsic part of the excursion. It expects people to relinquish the recognizable and adventure into the obscure, encouraging versatility and an eagerness to investigate additional opportunities. Opposing change can prompt stagnation, while embracing it makes the way for change and reestablishment.

Besides, the excursion is a continuum of encounters, each adding to the general embroidery of life. Wins and misfortunes, delights and distresses — all are woven into the texture of the excursion. It is through a comprehensive hug of these encounters that people gain a more profound comprehension of themselves, their qualities, and the significance they credit to their excursion.

In the domain of self-improvement, the unforeseen turns in the excursion act as cauldrons for character refinement. decisions even with affliction, the flexibility showed in testing minutes, and the ability to gain from misfortunes all add to the molding of character. These components are intelligent of individual development as well as impact the nature of connections and cooperations with the more extensive world.

The excursion's neglected regions reach out past the outside scenes to the inward domains of oneself. Self-disclosure is a ceaseless cycle, and the excursion gives sufficient chances to thoughtfulness and reflection. In snapshots of isolation or in the midst of life's difficulties, people frequently dig into the profundities of their own mind, unwinding layers of personality and understanding parts of themselves recently hid.

The investigation of internal regions includes going up against fears, recognizing weaknesses, and embracing the full range of feelings. An excursion into oneself requires mental fortitude, trustworthiness, and an eagerness to face viewpoints that might be awkward or new.

The compensations of this inside investigation are significant — a more profound association with one's true self and a more nuanced comprehension of individual inspirations and goals.

The unforeseen turns in the excursion might prompt experiences with assorted societies, convictions, and lifestyles. These social trades widen points of view, challenge suspicions, and cultivate a feeling of interconnectedness. Openness to neglected domains, whether physical or social, can be a groundbreaking encounter, separating boundaries and cultivating a more noteworthy appreciation for the variety of the human experience.

Besides, the excursion isn't static; it is a powerful course of development and development. As people explore through strange regions, they go through changes, shedding old characters and presumptions to clear a path for additional opportunities. This ceaseless course of restoration guarantees that the excursion stays energetic, offering new bits of knowledge and potential open doors for advancement.

Chasing after objectives and yearnings, the excursion's surprising turns might lead people to recalibrate their aspirations. What was once considered fundamental might lose its importance, and new interests might arise. These changes in context add to the developing idea of the excursion, underlining the significance of adaptability and a receptiveness to the changing scene of wants and needs.

The excursion's exciting bends in the road are not exclusively characterized by outside conditions but rather likewise by the inward stories people build. The narratives we educate ourselves regarding our encounters, difficulties, and victories shape the importance we get from the excursion. Changing the story, rethinking difficulties as any open doors, and developing a positive outlook add to a really improving and satisfying excursion.

As people cross the strange domains of the excursion, they might find a feeling of direction that rises above private desires. A reason driven life includes adjusting one's activities to a more noteworthy feeling of significance, adding to the prosperity of others or the improvement of society. This shift from self-centered goals to a more extensive, more charitable reason adds profundity and importance to the excursion.

The excursion's startling turns likewise brief people to analyze their relationship with time. The acknowledgment that life is limited and flighty can act as an impetus for a more purposeful and careful way to deal with using time effectively. Embracing the current second, enjoying encounters, and focusing on the main thing become core values in exploring the excursion.

Despite the obscure, the excursion welcomes people to develop a feeling of miracle and interest. The neglected regions hold secrets, valuable open doors for revelation, and the potential for stunning minutes.

Moving toward the excursion with an inquisitive mentality permits people to embrace the obscure with energy, cultivating a feeling of experience and an eagerness to investigate the profundities of plausibility.

Besides, the excursion's unforeseen turns frequently lead people to reevaluate their meanings of achievement and satisfaction. The cultural stories that recommend specific benchmarks of accomplishment might be tested, and people might address whether outside approvals line up with their inborn qualities. Reclassifying accomplishment based on one's conditions turns into a freeing try, considering a more credible and by and by significant excursion.

As the excursion unfurls, connections become necessary waymarkers on the way. The associations framed with family, companions, coaches, and even outsiders add to the extravagance of the excursion. Shared encounters, common help, and the bonds produced with others become persevering through parts of the account, featuring the significance of human associations in exploring the intricacies of life.

In the midst of vulnerability, the excursion frequently prompts people to develop a real feeling or otherworldliness. This might include an association with a higher power, an extending appreciation for the interconnectedness of all life, or a quest for significance past the material parts of presence. Otherworldly investigation turns into a wellspring of comfort and direction, giving a system to figuring out the secrets of the excursion.

In addition, the excursion's startling turns might lead people to face existential inquiries regarding the idea of life, the reason for presence, and the heritage they wish to abandon. Pondering these significant inquiries adds a layer of profundity to the excursion, empowering people to investigate the existential elements of their encounters and get importance from the transient idea of life.

The excursion is additionally set apart via times of thoughtfulness and times of outward investigation. There are times when people retreat into the safe-haven of self-reflection, looking for clearness in the midst of life's intricacies. These pondering minutes give a space to people to rethink their objectives, values, and yearnings, guaranteeing arrangement with their developing identity.

As people cross the neglected regions of the excursion, versatility turns into a crucial sidekick. Strength is the ability to quickly return from difficulties, adjust to difficulties, and continue on despite difficulty. The excursion's surprising turns might test people's flexibility, requesting a relentless obligation to their picked way and an enduring confidence in their capacity to beat hindrances.

In the domain of imagination and advancement, the excursion's unfamiliar regions act as rich ground for motivation. Imagination frequently flourishes notwithstanding oddity and eccentricism, provoking people to think outside the customary limits and investigate creative arrangements. The excursion turns into a material for imaginative articulation, welcoming people to add to the world in novel and extraordinary ways.

The excursion's unforeseen turns may likewise include times of isolation and independence. Isolation gives a space to reflection, self-revelation, and the development of internal strength. It is in snapshots of isolation that people might track down the lucidity to settle on vital choices, reconnect with their valid selves, and re-energize their spirits for the following period of the excursion.

Chasing neglected regions, the excursion frequently requires a harmony among arranging and suddenness. While vital arranging gives a guide to accomplishing objectives, the readiness to embrace immediacy considers fortunate revelations and the joining of unanticipated open doors into the story. This fragile dance among design and adaptability is fundamental in exploring the intricacies of the excursion.

The excursion's unforeseen turns might lead people to go up against fears and weaknesses. Whether it be dread of disappointment, apprehension about the obscure, or apprehension about weakness, tending to and defeating these feelings of trepidation turns into a groundbreaking part of the excursion. Defying fears makes the way for individual strengthening, self-assurance, and a more freed way to deal with exploring life's vulnerabilities.

Besides, the excursion is a demonstration of the intrinsic strength of the human soul. People have the ability to get through difficulties, adjust to evolving conditions, and rise up out of difficulties with newly discovered strength. The excursion turns into a story of win over difficulty, showing the unstoppable soul that drives people forward notwithstanding life's vulnerabilities.

In the domain of individual connections, the excursion's startling turns might include the back and forth movement of associations with others. Fellowships, heartfelt connections, and familial bonds go through changes as people develop and explore various periods of life. The capacity to explore these social movements with effortlessness, sympathy, and open correspondence is significant in supporting significant associations.

Besides, the excursion isn't bound to a straight movement; it incorporates patterns of development, stagnation, and reestablishment. There are times of overflow and times of shortage, seasons of satisfaction and seasons of distress. Perceiving the repeating idea of the excursion permits people to explore its intricacies with a feeling of composure, understanding that each stage adds to the general lavishness of the story.

The excursion's neglected domains may likewise include a retribution with mortality. Standing up to the fleetingness of life can be a sobering yet groundbreaking experience. It prompts people to live with a need to get going, to focus on the main thing, and to enjoy the current second. The familiarity with mortality turns into an impetus for a more deliberate and intentional excursion.

In the domain of individual character, the excursion's unforeseen turns might prompt the disclosure of dormant parts of oneself. As people explore through different encounters, they might uncover features of their character that were already unnoticed or underexplored. This constant course of self-revelation adds to a more nuanced comprehension of individual personality and credibility.

The excursion's unfamiliar domains additionally hold the potential for experiences with tutors and guides. These savvy people, whether as coaches, educators, or close friends, offer direction, backing, and significant bits of knowledge. Gaining from the insight of others turns into a critical part of the excursion, giving a compass to exploring neglected domains with more prominent insight and wisdom.

As people navigate the excursion, the quest for energy frequently arises as a directing power. Energy is the fuel that drives people forward, injecting their undertakings with excitement, commitment, and a feeling of direction. The arrangement of one's excursion with individual interests adds to a really satisfying and significant life, as people take part in pursuits that reverberate with their legitimate selves.

The excursion's unforeseen turns may likewise include times of rest and revival. Similarly as the regular world encounters patterns of lethargy and reestablishment, people benefit from snapshots of relief to re-energize their physical, close to home, and profound energies. Perceiving the significance of equilibrium and taking care of oneself is necessary in supporting the flexibility required for exploring the excursion.

In the domain of cultural commitments, the excursion's unknown regions might lead people to participate in demonstrations of administration and charitableness. The acknowledgment that the excursion is interconnected with the prosperity of others prompts people to add to the advancement of society. Thoughtful gestures, charity, and a promise to civil rights become necessary parts of a reason driven venture.

The excursion's startling turns may likewise include the route of moral situations and moral pickles. People are frequently stood up to with decisions that challenge their moral standards and values. Exploring these ethical scenes requires respectability, reflection, and a pledge to moral direct, guaranteeing that the excursion is lined up with a feeling of moral obligation.

Besides, the excursion's neglected regions might include a developing association with the normal world. The magnificence of nature, its cycles, and its perplexing biological systems become wellsprings of motivation and comfort. People might discover a significant feeling of association with the climate, cultivating a promise to ecological stewardship and manageability in the excursion.

Chasing neglected regions, the excursion welcomes people to embrace a development mentality. A development outlook is portrayed by a confidence in one's ability for learning and improvement. Embracing difficulties as any open doors for development, developing flexibility, and keeping an oddity for consistent learning add to a mentality that encourages individual and scholarly turn of events.

The excursion's unforeseen turns frequently lead people to address cultural standards and challenge the tried and true way of thinking. Basic assessment of winning philosophies and social stories turns into an intelligent practice in exploring the excursion with wisdom. This scholarly interest and ability to address add to the development of a free and informed point of view.

As people explore the excursion, the significance of self-empathy becomes obvious. The excursion's surprising turns might include snapshots of seen disappointment, difficulties, or individual weaknesses. Rehearsing self-empathy includes stretching out understanding and benevolence to oneself, recognizing

### 6.2 Exploration of diverse landscapes, cultures, and perspectives.

The investigation of different scenes, societies, and points of view is a groundbreaking excursion that rises above topographical limits and digs into the rich embroidery of human experience. A journey reaches out past the actual territory, enveloping the changed domains of social customs, cultural standards, and individual perspectives. As people set out on this investigation, they navigate various scenes as well as submerge themselves in the complexities of different societies and widen their viewpoints in significant ways.

Geologically, the investigation of assorted scenes includes wandering into territories that fluctuate from lavish rainforests to parched deserts, from transcending mountain reaches to broad beach front fields. Each scene holds its own novel magnificence, environmental frameworks, and regular miracles. The demonstration of investigating these different actual conditions permits people to observe the sensational excellence of the normal world and gain a more profound appreciation for the planet's biological variety.

Past the actual geology, social scenes offer a rich embroidery of customs, chronicles, and customs. The investigation of assorted societies includes drawing in with the traditions, customs, and lifestyles that shape the personalities of various networks.

It is a chance to commend the extravagance of human variety and perceive the ongoing ideas that interface us, encouraging a feeling of shared mankind.

Social investigation welcomes people to step into the shoes of others, to observe the world from alternate points of view, and to see the value in the variety of viewpoints that add to the human experience. It is an excursion of compassion, understanding, and diverse discourse that rises above generalizations and cultivates shared regard. This investigation of different societies turns into a scaffold that interfaces individuals, encouraging associations and separating the hindrances of misconception.

The investigation of assorted viewpoints reaches out past the limits of culture and includes the extraordinary perspectives of people formed by their encounters, convictions, and foundations. It includes a readiness to participate in discussions that challenge assumptions, to listen effectively to different voices, and to embrace the intricacy of contrasting conclusions. This investigation of points of view is a constant course of scholarly development, as people expand how they might interpret the world and refine their own perspectives through openness to different thoughts.

As people explore different scenes, they frequently end up amidst multicultural conditions that obscure the lines among topographical and social limits. Urban communities, for instance, become blends of assorted societies, where people from various foundations coincide and add to the dynamic embroidery of metropolitan life. This multicultural dynamism fills in as a microcosm of the more extensive investigation of different scenes and societies.

Besides, the investigation of different scenes, societies, and points of view frequently includes experiences with native networks whose lifestyles are complicatedly associated with the land they occupy. These people group convey significant information about feasible practices, environmental equilibrium, and an agreeable relationship with nature. Drawing in with native points of view offers a special focal point through which people can reexamine their own relationship with the climate and gather bits of knowledge into elective approaches to coinciding with the regular world.

The excursion through different scenes likewise unfurls in the domain of writing and human expression, giving an exceptional road to investigation. Writing, in its horde structures, fills in as a window into various societies and viewpoints, offering stories that rise above borders and give looks into the human condition. Imaginative articulations, whether in visual expressions, music, or dance, become strong mediums through which people can submerge themselves in the imaginative soul of different societies.

The investigation of different scenes, societies, and points of view isn't simply a physical or scholarly undertaking; it is likewise a profoundly close to home and otherworldly excursion.

The experiences with various lifestyles summon a scope of feelings — from the stunningness motivated by normal miracles to the compassion inspired by shared human stories. An excursion resounds on a profound level, inciting people to consider their own qualities, needs, and associations with the world.

In the domain of social investigation, celebrations and festivities become windows into the core of assorted networks. Partaking in these social celebrations permits people to encounter the delight, solidarity, and customs that characterize various social orders. Whether it's the energetic shades of Holi in India, the musical beats of Festival in Brazil, or the seriousness of Dia de los Muertos in Mexico, social festivals give vivid encounters that rise above language obstructions and proposition a more profound comprehension of the social texture.

Culinary investigation is one more essential feature of the excursion through assorted societies. Food fills in as a widespread language that rises above borders, and each culinary practice conveys the flavors, fragrances, and accounts of a specific culture. Investigating assorted foods includes appreciating new preferences as well as grasping the verifiable, social, and social settings that have molded the culinary customs of various areas.

The investigation of assorted scenes, societies, and points of view frequently drives people to defy issues of civil rights and value. Openness to various cultural standards and designs prompts reflection on fundamental imbalances, separation, and basic freedoms issues. It turns into a source of inspiration, encouraging people to advocate for positive change, challenge severe frameworks, and add to making an additional fair and comprehensive world.

Going through different scenes permits people to observe firsthand the effect of natural changes and the significance of economical practices. Whether it's the softening ice sheets in polar districts, deforestation in tropical rainforests, or the outcomes of urbanization on neighborhood biological systems, the investigation of different scenes turns into an obvious sign of the interconnectedness between human exercises and the soundness of the planet.

The excursion through assorted points of view likewise includes wrestling with the intricacies of history. Many scenes bear the engravings of authentic occasions, from antiquated civic establishments to later battles for autonomy and civil rights. Investigating authentic destinations and drawing in with the accounts of various networks extends' comprehension people might interpret the intricacies and heritages that shape this present reality.

Also, the investigation of assorted viewpoints provokes people to go up against their own predispositions and suppositions. It is a chance for contemplation, mindfulness, and self-improvement. Perceiving the limits of one's own point of view and effectively trying to expand one's figuring out encourages a more comprehensive and receptive way to deal with the world.

In the advanced age, the investigation of assorted scenes, societies, and points of view reaches out past actual travel. The virtual world gives a stage to people to associate with individuals from various pieces of the globe, participate in multifaceted discourse, and access an abundance of data about different societies. Web-based entertainment, online discussions, and computerized narrating add to a worldwide trade of thoughts and viewpoints.

Language turns into a critical device in the investigation of different societies and points of view. Learning various dialects opens ways to more profound social comprehension, works with significant correspondence, and cultivates associations with people from different phonetic foundations. The capacity to explore etymological variety upgrades the lavishness of the investigation, empowering people to connect all the more really with the networks they experience.

In the domain of training, the investigation of different points of view is essential to encouraging a balanced and universally mindful populace. Instructive educational plans that consolidate different voices, chronicles, and social viewpoints add to a more comprehensive and impartial learning climate. Openness to different points of view in instructive settings gets ready people to explore the intricacies of a globalized world.

The investigation of different scenes, societies, and points of view isn't without its difficulties. Social contrasts might prompt misconceptions, language hindrances might present correspondence leaps, and exploring new scenes might introduce strategic troubles. Notwithstanding, it is exactly in defeating these difficulties that people foster flexibility, versatility, and multifaceted skill.

The excursion through different scenes and societies is additionally a solicitation to natural stewardship. Seeing the delicacy of biological systems and the effect of human exercises on the climate urges people to think about their natural impression. It turns into a call to embrace maintainable practices, support protection endeavors, and add to the conservation of the planet for people in the future.

In the domain of social investigation, moral contemplations come to the very front. Regarding the customs, convictions, and practices of various societies requires a careful and socially touchy methodology. Moral travel includes cognizant decisions that limit adverse consequences on nearby networks, advance dependable the travel industry, and encourage common regard among explorers and host societies.

**6.3 The protagonist confronts personal biases and broadens their worldview.**

The hero's process is a significant investigation that rises above the physical and digs into the profundities of self-revelation. At the core of this extraordinary odyssey lies the difficult and essential showdown of individual inclinations. An excursion requires boldness, thoughtfulness, and an eagerness to address imbued convictions, making ready for the expanding of the hero's perspective.

The underlying phases of the story find the hero working inside the limits of their laid out conviction framework. These inclinations, frequently formed by social, cultural, or individual impacts, go about as a focal point through which they see the world. The excursion starts with an acknowledgment of these predispositions, a pivotal step that makes way for the hero's development.

Facing individual inclinations is definitely not an agreeable cycle. It requests an eagerness to investigate one's own contemplations, convictions, and biases. The hero wrestles with the distress that emerges from recognizing the presence of inclinations, as well as the acknowledgment that these predispositions might have incidentally impacted their activities and cooperations.

The outside world fills in as a proving ground for the hero's developing mindfulness. Collaborations with different characters and openness to differentiating points of view become essential minutes in the story. These experiences go about as mirrors, reflecting parts of the hero's predispositions that might have recently slipped through the cracks. The course of a conflict is definitely not a one-time occasion yet a continuous discourse with oneself, unfurling steadily with each new experience.

The excursion towards standing up to individual inclinations includes a sensitive dance among weakness and versatility. The hero might confront snapshots of distress, mental discord, or even protection from change. In any case, it is through this weakness that development becomes conceivable. The eagerness to challenge one's own suspicions and participate in awkward discussions turns into an impetus for the hero's very own change.

Social inundation turns into a critical part of the hero's excursion. Openness to various social standards, customs, and lifestyles turns into a rich embroidery through which inclinations are unwound. The hero wrestles with the acknowledgment that their perspective isn't widespread, and the variety of human encounters difficulties the limitation of their recently held convictions.

Amidst social submersion, the hero experiences characters who act as impetuses for change. These might be people who typify viewpoints that straightforwardly challenge the hero's predispositions or the individuals who, through their accounts and encounters, give elective stories. These characters become guides, inciting the hero to address, learn, and advance.

The excursion towards facing individual predispositions isn't exclusively an outer investigation yet in addition an inside uncovering. The hero digs into the foundations of their convictions, following them back to developmental encounters, cultural impacts, or acquired belief systems. This thoughtful interaction includes a reexamination of values, a reevaluation of biases, and a promise to forgetting hurtful thought processes.

As the hero wrestles with the intricacies of standing up to individual inclinations, they might encounter snapshots of mental discord. The cacophony emerges from the contention between existing convictions and new, problematic data. This uneasiness turns into a cauldron for change, pushing the hero to accommodate irregularities and adjust their convictions to a more nuanced and comprehensive point of view.

The story unfurls as a mosaic of encounters, each adding to the hero's steady development. Going through different scenes and drawing in with a bunch of societies turns into an illustration for the sweeping excursion inside. The outer investigation reflects the inward mission for understanding, and the hero discovers that the lavishness of the world is reflected in the intricacy of human idea.

The hero's connections go through a transformation as they explore the territory of individual inclination. Companionships and associations that were once based on shared predispositions might be tried, and the hero wrestles with the subject of validness in their connections. A few associations might crack, while others extend because of common development and a common obligation to facing predispositions.

The account additionally investigates the effect of force elements on private predispositions. The hero perceives that cultural designs, authentic heritages, and foundational imbalances add to the development and propagation of inclinations. Defying individual predispositions in this way becomes weaved with a more extensive consciousness of civil rights issues, provoking the hero to think about their part in destroying severe frameworks.

All through the excursion, the hero learns the craft of undivided attention. This ability becomes instrumental in expanding their perspective. By really paying attention to the accounts and encounters of others, the hero acquires bits of knowledge that challenge their suspicions. The demonstration of listening turns into an extension that interfaces different viewpoints, encouraging compassion and understanding.

The hero's a conflict of individual predispositions is certainly not a direct direction however a repeating interaction. There might be snapshots of relapse, where old predispositions reemerge, requiring reestablished reflection and obligation to change. These repetitive examples mirror the intricacies of self-improvement and the continuous idea of the excursion towards a more comprehensive perspective.

Training assumes an essential part in the hero's development. Openness to different writing, verifiable records, and instructive assets turns into a wellspring of edification. The hero draws in with materials that give elective stories, challenge verifiable bends, and deal a more extensive comprehension of the intricacies implanted in cultural designs.

As the hero goes up against individual predispositions, they wrestle with the idea of honor. Recognizing one's honor turns into a necessary piece of the excursion, provoking the hero to perceive the benefits they might have delighted in and the obligation that accompanies it. The investigation of honor adds one more layer to the's comprehension hero might interpret foundational imbalances.

The account investigates the convergences of personality and inclination. The hero perceives that their own character — whether formed by race, orientation, financial status, or different variables — meets with their inclinations. This nuanced investigation prompts a more profound comprehension of the manners by which individual encounters cross with cultural designs to shape individual points of view.

The hero's a conflict of individual predispositions stretches out past individual change to aggregate activity. Perceiving the effect of aggregate predispositions on underestimated networks, the hero turns into a promoter for social change. This promotion includes testing prejudicial works on, enhancing minimized voices, and effectively partaking in endeavors to make an all the more and impartial society.

The excursion towards expanding the hero's perspective likewise includes a recalibration of their ethical compass. The hero explores moral predicaments, scrutinizing the moral establishments whereupon their past convictions might have been assembled. This moral recalibration turns into a core value for the hero's activities, underscoring the significance of adjusting individual qualities to a guarantee to equity and value.

The story unfurls against the setting of cultural change. The hero's very own process crosses with more extensive developments for social change, underscoring the interconnectedness of individual and aggregate development. The hero perceives their job inside the more extensive setting of cultural movements, adding to an additional comprehensive and humane world.

The hero's a conflict of individual inclinations is set apart by snapshots of modesty. The readiness to concede when they are off-base, to gain from botches, and to embrace a position of ceaseless development turns into a sign of the hero's advancing person. This modesty is definitely not an indication of shortcoming yet a strength that permits the hero to explore the intricacies of individual change with elegance.

Otherworldly investigation becomes interlaced with the hero's a showdown of individual inclinations. The excursion towards a more comprehensive perspective isn't exclusively savvy yet in addition includes a more profound comprehension of interconnectedness and shared humankind. This otherworldly aspect adds a significant layer to the story, featuring the extraordinary force of sympathy and empathy.

The story additionally investigates the job of local area in the hero's excursion. Strong people group give spaces to the hero to share their advancing viewpoints, gain from others, and get consolation during snapshots of challenge. These people group become a wellspring of solidarity, supporting that the excursion towards standing up to individual predispositions isn't embraced in disconnection.

The hero's extended perspective isn't without its difficulties. The account investigates the obstruction and pushback the hero might look from the people who are dug in their own predispositions. These moves become open doors for the hero to improve their backing abilities, take part in helpful discourse, and become problem solvers inside their authoritative reaches.

In the last phases of the story, the hero arises changed — a person with a more extensive perspective, an uplifted feeling of compassion, and a guarantee to continuous development. The excursion towards facing individual inclinations turns into a demonstration of the hero's versatility, boldness, and limit with regards to positive change.

# Chapter 7

**Resurrection and Redemption**

In the immense region of human life, the topics of revival and recovery have woven an embroidery that traverses the records of history, writing, and the human mind. These ideas, loaded down with significant importance, have risen above social and worldly limits, making a permanent imprint on the shared mindset of mankind.

Restoration, at its center, epitomizes the possibility of recovery and recharging — a takeoff from the grip of death or misery, a resurrection into another presence. The idea tracks down its foundations in strict accounts, where figures come back to life, representing the victory of life over mortality. Christianity, with its foundation confidence in the restoration of Jesus Christ, exemplifies this subject. The tale of Christ's restoration fills in as a strong purposeful anecdote for trust, recharging, and the commitment of an otherworldly presence past the human curl.

Past strict settings, the idea of revival penetrates writing, folklore, and social customs. In different fantasies and legends, legends and champions beat demise or misfortune, arising out of the remains of their previous selves. The phoenix, a legendary bird that consistently combusts and rises once more from its remains, encapsulates this everlasting pattern of death and resurrection, representing strength and change.

Artistic works have dove into the intricacies of restoration, investigating the actual return from death as well as the revival of spirits, dreams, and goals. Mary Shelley's "Frankenstein" wrestles with the results of resurrecting the dead, scrutinizing the moral and moral ramifications of assuming the part of the Maker. The original raises piercing requests about the restrictions of human aspiration and the obligation that accompanies the ability to revive.

Restoration, be that as it may, stretches out past the domain of the powerful and allegorical. It frequently appears in the commonplace, regular encounters of people exploring the maze of life. Individuals defy mishaps, disappointments, and individual emergencies, just to rise again with recently discovered strength and shrewdness. The human limit with regards to strength and restoration reflects the general subject of revival, exhibiting that, on a microcosmic scale, resurrection is an inborn part of the human condition.

Lined up with the subject of revival is the idea of reclamation — a mind boggling process that includes compensation, pardoning, and the rebuilding of one's personality or status. Reclamation suggests an excursion from haziness to light, from offense to salvation, and from moral rot to otherworldly restoration. This subject reverberates across societies, religions, and philosophical systems, representing a widespread human longing for fresh opportunities and the chance of change.

Strict customs frequently stress the significance of reclamation as a way to profound salvation. In Christianity, the idea is entwined with the story of wrongdoing and the redemptive force of heavenly effortlessness. The tale of the intemperate child, for example, typifies the embodiment of recovery — an unpredictable soul tracking down pardoning and compromise after getting back to the generous hug of an easy-going dad.

Past strict settings, writing has investigated reclamation as a focal theme, introducing characters who go through significant change through their battles and preliminaries. Charles Dickens' "A Story of Two Urban communities" winds around a story that navigates the wild scenes of the French Upheaval. The personality of Sydney Container, at first portrayed as loose and without reason, goes through a redemptive bend that comes full circle in a self-conciliatory demonstration, representing a definitive reclamation through adoration and penance.

Recovery isn't bound to the domain of fiction; it penetrates genuine accounts as people wrestle with individual evil spirits, cultural assumptions, and the outcomes of their decisions.

The human experience is overflowing with accounts of people who, in spite of confronting affliction and moral downfalls, leave on excursions of self-disclosure and change, looking for recovery according to themselves as well as other people.

The crossing point of revival and recovery is especially convincing, as it investigates the unpredictable interchange among death and resurrection, sin and salvation, misery and trust. The excursion toward recovery frequently requires a figurative or otherworldly revival — a shedding of the old self and the rise of a reestablished, illuminated being.

In looking at these topics, it becomes obvious that they are not secluded ideas but rather interconnected strands in the unpredictable trap of the human experience. The repeating idea of life, demise, and resurrection reflects the unending battle for reclamation — a mission for importance, reason, and the compromise of one's past with the conceivable outcomes representing things to come.

The creative domain, including visual expressions, music, and film, has likewise been a rich ground for the investigation of revival and recovery. Craftsmen, artists, and movie producers utilize their picked mediums to portray the human condition, imbuing their manifestations with the intricacies of life's battles and the potential for greatness.

Think about the visual expressions, where artworks and figures frequently catch the substance of revival and recovery. Strict show-stoppers, like Michelangelo's "The Last Judgment" or Leonardo da Vinci's "The Restoration," epitomize the heavenly and natural elements of these subjects, welcoming watchers to examine the interaction among transgression and salvation, demise and resurrection.

Also, the domain of music reverberates with pieces that dive into the close to home subtleties of restoration and reclamation. From traditional orchestras to contemporary ditties, artists have utilized tune and verses to inspire the extraordinary force of reclamation and the confident notes of revival. The redemptive curve is obvious in the taking off crescendos and powerful harmonies that reverberation the human excursion from gloom to win.

Film, with its visual narrating ability, has rejuvenated stories that unpredictably weave the strings of revival and recovery. Movies, for example, "The Shawshank Recovery" and "The Green Mile" investigate the extraordinary force of reclamation inside the limits of the jail framework, depicting characters who track down comfort and recharging in spite of the grimness of their conditions. The revival of trust and the recovery of the human soul become focal themes, resounding with crowds on an instinctive level.

The interest with these subjects stretches out past the domains of workmanship and writing; it pervades philosophical talk and moral contemplations.

Savants over the entire course of time have wrestled with inquiries of profound quality, equity, and the potential for individual and cultural reclamation. The investigation of these topics raises key requests about human instinct, unrestrained choice, and the limit with respect to moral development.

In the philosophical scene, existentialist scholars, for example, Jean-Paul Sartre and Albert Camus pondered the intrinsic ridiculousness of life and the mission for importance in an apparently unconcerned universe. While their viewpoints fluctuated, both recognized the existential battle for genuineness and the chance of recovery through individual decisions and activities.

The convergence of revival and recovery additionally tracks down reverberation in moral conversations. The thought of pardoning, reparation, and the chance of reclamation assumes an essential part in forming cultural mentalities toward equity and restoration. The law enforcement framework, for example, is frequently gone up against with the test of offsetting correctional measures with the potential for the recovery and reclamation of guilty parties.

In the woven artwork of human connections, the topics of revival and reclamation manifest in the elements of pardoning and compromise. Relational struggles, treacheries, and cracks in connections should be visible as occurrences of profound passing, where the chance of restoration depends on the readiness of people to look for recovery and remake associations. The demonstration of pardoning, an impetus for reclamation, turns into a strong power in mending injured spirits and cultivating development.

The investigation of revival and reclamation takes on an impactful aspect with regards to verifiable stories and aggregate memory. Social orders wrestle with the traditions of past abominations, wars, and shameful acts, looking for roads for mending and recovery. The most common way of recognizing verifiable wrongs, offering compensations, and cultivating compromise mirrors an aggregate longing for cultural restoration — a takeoff from the shadows of a disturbed past toward a more brilliant, all the more future.

As mankind goes up against the heap difficulties of the contemporary world, the topics of restoration and reclamation reverberate with recharged criticalness. Worldwide emergencies, cultural breaks, and ecological worries highlight the requirement for extraordinary change and the chance of an aggregate restoration — a resurrection of values, cognizance, and a common obligation to the prosperity of the planet and its occupants.

The appearance of innovation and the interconnectedness of the cutting edge world have introduced new aspects to the investigation of these subjects. The computerized age, with its quick speed of progress and data over-burden, presents difficulties to people and social orders the same.

The mission for significance and reason in a mechanically determined world repeats the immortal human longing for restoration — a recovery of direction and a greatness of the ordinary.

The computerized domain itself turns into a figurative scene for restoration and reclamation. Virtual entertainment stages, for example, offer people the open door to arrange and introduce their characters, displaying snapshots of individual victory, development, and versatility. The virtual space turns into a material for the development of computerized stories that reflect the well established topics of defeating difficulty and looking for recovery according to a worldwide crowd.

All the while, the computerized scene presents difficulties that require aggregate flexibility and cultural recovery. Issues like internet based poisonousness, deception, and the disintegration of security highlight the more obscure parts of the computerized age. The recovery of the computerized domain requires moral contemplations, capable use, and the aggregate obligation to making a virtual space that cultivates positive development and certified association.

In considering the subjects of restoration and recovery, recognizing the variety of human encounters and perspectives is fundamental. Social varieties, strict convictions, and individual translations enhance the embroidery of these topics, offering a multicolored perspective on the human excursion. The comprehensiveness of these ideas lies not in an unbending, solitary story but rather in the heap ways people and social orders explore the intricacies of life, passing, and the unending journey for reestablishment.

The investigation of restoration and reclamation welcomes thoughtfulness into the individual and aggregate accounts that shape the human experience. It prompts people to go up against their own snapshots of misery, recognize the chance of change, and think about the ways to recovery accessible inside the embroidered artwork of their lives. All the while, it approaches social orders to wrestle with verifiable treacheries, cultivate compromise, and imagine a future that embraces the potential for aggregate restoration.

As the human story unfurls, the topics of restoration and reclamation persevere as ageless themes that rise above the limits of time, culture, and philosophy. They resound as reverberations of the human soul's getting through limit with respect to reestablishment, development, and the unending mission for significance in the perplexing embroidery of presence.

### 7.1 The protagonist faces the ultimate challenge or adversary.

In the huge domain of narrating, the hero confronting a definitive test or enemy remains as an immortal story model, a pot that tests the backbone of characters and unwinds the substance of their excursion. This urgent second, frequently the peak of a story, fills in as a pot where the hero defies the summit of their preliminaries, an imposing enemy, or an unrealistic impediment that stretches them to the edges of their capacities and convictions.

At the core of this model lies the legend's excursion, a story structure tracked down in fantasies, sagas, and stories crossing societies and ages. Joseph Campbell's monomyth, a calculated structure for the legend's excursion, frames a succession of stages that heroes go through, coming full circle in a climactic showdown with a definitive test or foe. This repeating design mirrors the widespread human experience of confronting preliminaries, beating affliction, and accomplishing individual change.

One of the principal traits of this story model is the intrinsic strain between the hero and the imposing power they defy. This power might appear as an exacting bad guy — a reprobate with odious goals — or as a figurative foe, like a conflict under the surface, existential predicament, or an outside impediment that appears to be inconceivable. The idea of this challenge fluctuates across kinds and stories, traversing from the fantastical domains of folklore to the abrasive scenes of reasonable fiction.

In legendary stories, like Homer's "The Iliad" or Virgil's "The Aeneid," a definitive test frequently appears as a legendary animal, a vindictive divinity, or a strong enemy on the front line. The legend, be it Achilles or Aeneas, faces preliminaries that request actual ability as well as moral boldness and flexibility. These stories investigate the intricacies of courage, digging into the penances and decisions made despite apparently impossible chances.

In the domain of imagination writing, J.R.R. Tolkien's "The Master of the Rings" offers a quintessential illustration of the hero defying a definitive test. Frodo Baggins, the impossible legend, worries about the concern of the One Ring and should explore the tricky landscape of Mordor to obliterate it. The climactic showdown at Mount Destruction addresses an actual battle against dim powers as well as an inner fight against the tainting impact of force.

Moving past the domains of folklore and dream, the model of the hero confronting a definitive test tracks down reverberation in contemporary and sensible fiction. In Fyodor Dostoevsky's "Wrongdoing and Discipline," the hero, Raskolnikov, wrestles with the results of his ethically equivocal activities, prompting a mental and existential showdown that fills in as the peak of the story. A definitive test, in this unique situation, is the hero's a showdown with his own heart and the quest for recovery.

Likewise, in Harper Lee's "To Kill a Mockingbird," Atticus Finch stands up to a definitive test as he protects Tom Robinson, an African American man wrongly blamed for assault, in a racially charged Southern town. The ill-disposed powers incorporate instilled bias, social foul play, and the intricacies of the general set of laws. Atticus' unfaltering obligation to equity and ethical quality characterizes the zenith of the account, displaying the mental fortitude expected to stand up to foundational foul play.

The paradigm expands its venture into artistic narrating, where heroes face a definitive test on the cinema. In Christopher Nolan's "The Dull Knight," Batman (Bruce Wayne) defies the Joker, a tumultuous power that challenges the legend's ethical code and drives Gotham City to the edge. A definitive test rises above simple actual showdown; it digs into the moral and philosophical elements of chivalry, penance, and the decisions that characterize the hero.

In sci-fi, a definitive test frequently arises as existential dangers or tragic situations. In Aldous Huxley's "State-of-the-art existence," the hero, John the Savage, faces a general public without singularity and mankind. His definitive test is to oppose similarity and keep up with his identity in a dehumanizing world. The story investigates the conflict among uniqueness and cultural standards, stressing the hero's battle for legitimacy notwithstanding a conventionalist oppressed world.

The model of the hero confronting a definitive test isn't restricted to conventional stories. In computer games, players frequently expect the job of a hero exploring virtual universes full of difficulties. Games like "The Legend of Zelda: Ocarina of Time" or "Dull Spirits" present heroes with considerable foes, complex riddles, and amazing fights that act as the summit of the player's excursion. The intelligent idea of gaming adds a special aspect to the model, permitting players to submerge themselves in the hero's battle and win.

Past writing, film, and gaming, the model of the hero confronting a definitive test saturates other imaginative articulations, including theater, music, and visual expressions. Shakespearean misfortunes, for example, "Hamlet" or "Macbeth," exhibit heroes standing up to a definitive test, be it the intricacies of vengeance, political desire, or existential gloom. In music, idea collections frequently recount accounts of heroes exploring difficulties, with climactic tracks filling in as the story summit. Visual specialists catch the embodiment of this paradigm through canvases and models that portray gallant figures in the pains of unequivocal showdowns.

The persevering through allure of this story paradigm lies in its impression of the human condition. It reverberates with crowds since it reflects the general insight of confronting misfortune, pursuing decisions in the cauldron of difficulties, and going through groundbreaking excursions. Whether in the legendary scenes of old stories or the contemporary settings of practical fiction, the paradigm addresses the perpetual journey for importance, flexibility, and the victory of the human soul.

A fundamental component of this account structure is the hero's development and change all through the excursion. A definitive test turns into a pot for character improvement, compelling the hero to face their feelings of trepidation, defects, and inward devils. This change isn't exclusively physical or outside; it includes the advancement of the hero's convictions, values, and comprehension of the world.

Consider the exemplary legend's process framed by Joseph Campbell, where the hero sets out on a mission, faces preliminaries and difficulties, and at last goes through a course of self-disclosure and illumination. A definitive test fills in as the nexus of this groundbreaking excursion, the place where the hero's real essence is uncovered, and their strength is tried. Whether it's the magnanimous boldness of a knight confronting a winged serpent or the ethical courage of an individual standing up to cultural shamefulness, a definitive test takes shape the substance of the legend's development.

Also, the prime example takes into account nuanced investigation of moral and moral predicaments. A definitive test frequently gives heroes decisions that rise above simple endurance or triumph. These decisions epitomize the ethical texture of the account, constraining characters and crowds the same to wrestle with inquiries of good and bad, penance, and everyone's benefit. The hero turns into a vessel through which these moral contemplations are inspected, adding layers of profundity and intricacy to the narrating.

The goal of a definitive test, whether through win or misfortune, reverberates with crowds on a profound level. The therapy experienced by watchers or perusers is a demonstration of the force of narrating to summon compassion, association, and a common perspective of the human experience. A definitive test turns into a cauldron for the hero as well as for the crowd, welcoming reflection on their own battles, decisions, and limit with regards to flexibility.

In looking at explicit models across different mediums, it becomes apparent that the paradigm of the hero confronting a definitive test rises above social, worldly, and classification limits. From old legends to contemporary blockbusters, from traditional writing to intelligent gaming, the story structure perseveres as an essential component of narrating. Its omnipresence highlights its importance as an impression of human desires, fears, and the persevering through confidence in the groundbreaking capability of difficulty.

The reverberation of this model likewise reaches out to its versatility and reevaluation across different accounts. While the center components stay steady — preliminary, conflict, change — the logical subtleties shift in view of the class, social background, and topical focal point of the story. A legend confronting a legendary monster in old Greece might have the equivalent essential design with a cutting edge wannabe testing cultural standards, yet the story particulars mirror the unmistakable worries and upsides of their separate settings.

All in all, the paradigm of the hero confronting a definitive test or foe remains as a demonstration of the persevering through force of narrating to catch the intricacies of the human experience. It fills in as a story cauldron, where characters stand up to their most profound feelings of trepidation, pursue decisions that characterize their pith, and go through groundbreaking excursions that resound with crowds across time and culture. As narrating proceeds to develop and adjust, this original remaining parts a central support point, welcoming crowds to submerge themselves in the perpetual journey for importance, strength, and the victory of the human soul.

**7.2 Application of lessons learned and growth achieved throughout the journey.**

The story circular segment of any convincing story, whether it unfurls in writing, film, or reality, frequently finishes in a period of reflection and application — the utilization of examples learned and the development accomplished all through the excursion. This stage fills in as an extension between the hero's extraordinary encounters and the mix of those encounters into their present and future selves. It is a critical second where the collected insight, freshly discovered abilities, and developed viewpoints are scrutinized in the cauldron of commonsense application.

This topical investigation stretches out past the limits of fiction into the domains of self-awareness, training, and expert life. With regards to self-awareness, people go through different encounters that shape their personality, values, and comprehension of the world. Whether through wins, difficulties, or snapshots of self-revelation, these encounters add to a supply of information and experiences that can be applied in exploring future difficulties.

Consider the exemplary legend's excursion, a story layout that has persevered through hundreds of years and societies. The legend, having confronted preliminaries, faced enemies, and gone through a course of change, remains at the edge of another section — the utilization of illustrations learned. This frequently includes the legend getting back to their normal world with freshly discovered information or gifts, prepared to add to the advancement of their local area or the goal of waiting struggles.

In writing, the use of examples gained is obvious in works going from antiquated sagas to contemporary books. In Homer's "The Odyssey," for example, Odysseus sets out on an excursion loaded up with hardships prior to getting back. The use of illustrations learned is exemplified in his essential clever and flexibility as he explores difficulties, at last recovering his realm and reestablishing request.

Present day writing additionally investigates this topic. In Khaled Hosseini's "The Kite Sprinter," the hero, Amir, wrestles with responsibility and recovery all through his life. The use of illustrations learned happens as he stands up to the results of his past activities, looks for recovery, and tries to set things right. The account highlights the extraordinary force of self-reflection and the cognizant work to apply freshly discovered intelligence.

Past the domain of fiction, the use of examples learned is a foundation of instruction. Understudies participate in a constant course of getting the hang of, acclimatizing data, and applying procured information to take care of issues or explore certifiable difficulties. The instructive excursion, whether in conventional scholarly settings or through experiential learning, underlines the significance of functional application as a proportion of genuine comprehension.

In proficient settings, the use of examples learned is basic to individual and authoritative development. Experts frequently experience complex situations that request versatility, critical thinking abilities, and the capacity to draw on previous encounters. The information acquired from the two victories and disappointments turns into an important asset, molding dynamic cycles and impacting key ways to deal with difficulties.

Initiative advancement programs, for instance, center around the utilization of illustrations figured out how to upgrade authority abilities. Pioneers ponder previous encounters, break down their administration styles, and carry out changes to work on their viability. This iterative course of learning and application adds to the advancement of initiative abilities over the long run.

Besides, the domain of self-awareness puts areas of strength for an on applying illustrations gained from different educational encounters. People go through self-disclosure, go up against fears, and explore connections, all of which add to their self-improvement. The capacity to apply these examples in various settings cultivates the capacity to appreciate people on a profound level, flexibility, and a more profound comprehension of oneself as well as other people.

The topical investigation of the use of examples learned reverberates across social and philosophical practices. In Eastern ways of thinking, for example, Buddhism, the idea of care and mindfulness fills in as an establishment for the use of illustrations gained from one second to another. The development of astuteness through lived encounters and the cognizant utilization of that insight in day to day existence line up with the more extensive ethos of these practices.

According to a mental point of view, scholars, for example, Jean Piaget and Lev Vygotsky underline the significance of experiential learning and the utilization of information in mental turn of events. Piaget's phases of mental improvement feature the continuous movement from concrete functional reasoning to formal functional reasoning, wherein people gain the ability to think uniquely and apply information in a more summed up way.

In the domain of relational connections, the use of illustrations learned becomes urgent for cultivating better associations. People explore the intricacies of human collaboration, gaining from previous oversights and triumphs in correspondence, compassion, and compromise. The use of the capacity to appreciate anyone on a deeper level, acquired through mindfulness and reflection, adds to the development of significant connections.

This topical string stretches out into the texture of regular daily existence, where people persistently apply examples learned in exploring the complexities of work, family, and individual undertakings. Life's difficulties act as impetuses for development, inciting people to draw on their repository of encounters and bits of knowledge to beat deterrents and settle on informed choices.

Moreover, the utilization of illustrations learned is interwoven with flexibility — the capacity to quickly return from misfortune and arise more grounded. Versatility isn't just a characteristic however a powerful interaction that includes gaining from difficulties, adjusting to change, and applying recently discovered strength and information to confront future difficulties. This recurrent course of encountering, learning, and applying adds to the iterative idea of individual and aggregate strength.

In authoritative settings, the utilization of illustrations learned takes on essential importance. After critical undertakings, drives, or emergencies, associations take part in posthumous examinations to gather experiences and recognize regions for development. The use of these examples illuminates future procedures, risk relief plans, and hierarchical advancement drives, adding to a culture of consistent improvement.

An outstanding illustration of the utilization of examples learned in the hierarchical setting is the field of undertaking the executives. Project supervisors lead present venture audits on evaluate what functioned admirably, what turned out badly, and how future activities can profit from these experiences. This intelligent practice guarantees that the association advances and adjusts in view of pragmatic encounters, improving generally project achievement rates.

The use of illustrations learned is likewise clear in the field of development. Trailblazers and business people frequently face the overwhelming assignment of exploring vulnerabilities, disappointments, and market elements. The capacity to apply bits of knowledge acquired from past endeavors, regardless of whether effective, adds to the spryness and versatility of people and associations in the quickly changing scene of development.

In the always developing universe of innovation, the use of illustrations learned is vital to headways and leap forwards. Researchers and designers expand on past revelations, gain from bombed explores, and apply their insight to push the limits of what is conceivable. The iterative idea of logical request depends on the constant utilization of examples figured out how to refine speculations, tests, and mechanical developments.

In rundown, the topical investigation of the utilization of illustrations learned highlights its universality across assorted features of life. Whether in writing, training, self-awareness, or expert undertakings, people and associations participate in a repeating cycle of encountering, reflecting, and applying information acquired from previous encounters.

This powerful interchange among hypothesis and practice, among insight and application, enhances the texture of the human experience and adds to the continuous excursion of development and improvement.

### 7.3 Redemption and emergence as a transformed individual.

The idea of reclamation, profoundly implanted in human stories and social structures, resounds as a strong theme addressing the potential for change and recharging. Reclamation, in its embodiment, suggests the compensation for past offenses, the recovering of one's ethical standing, and the development as a changed person. This significant topic navigates the domains of writing, religion, reasoning, and individual stories, offering an immortal investigation of the human limit with respect to change and development.

In strict customs, recovery frequently conveys a holy undertone, mirroring the heavenly or powerful demonstration of salvation. Christianity, specifically, puts a focal accentuation on recovery through the conciliatory demonstration of Jesus Christ. The story of Christ's torturous killing and restoration represents a definitive recovery — a help from above that offers salvation and pardon for humankind's wrongdoings. The Christian story highlights the groundbreaking force of reclamation, welcoming devotees to look for recharging and embrace a way of uprightness.

Past strict settings, writing has long wrestled with the subject of recovery, investigating the intricacies of individual and moral change. Exemplary works, for example, Charles Dickens' "A Story of Two Urban communities" or Victor Hugo's "Les Misérables" portray characters who go through significant excursions of reclamation. In Dickens' novel, Sydney Container's self-conciliatory demonstration turns into the encapsulation of reclamation, featuring the potential for moral revival even notwithstanding cultural commotion. Essentially, Jean Valjean's change from a solidified criminal to a big-hearted force for good exemplifies the redemptive bend in Hugo's magnum opus.

Present day writing keeps on diving into the complexities of recovery, frequently depicting characters who wrestle with their own ethical issues and look for a way to restoration. Khaled Hosseini's "The Kite Sprinter" investigates the topics of culpability and recovery as the hero, Amir, faces the results of double-crossing his cherished, lifelong companion. The novel dives into the intricacies of moral obligation and the potential for reclamation through demonstrations of boldness and penance.

In the domain of reasoning, existentialist scholars, for example, Jean-Paul Sartre and Albert Camus contemplate the idea of reclamation with regards to individual opportunity and obligation. Sartre's idea of "dishonesty" features the manners in which people misdirect themselves and try not to get a sense of ownership with their activities. Recovery, in the existentialist system, includes a cognizant affirmation of one's opportunity and the bona fide quest for a significant presence.

Individual accounts likewise give testimony regarding the groundbreaking force of recovery. People confronting individual emergencies, enslavement, or moral downfalls frequently set out on excursions of self-revelation and recovery. The interaction includes a profound reflection, a retribution with previous oversights, and a pledge to positive change. Recuperation programs for compulsion, for example, underline the significance of recognizing wrongs, offering to set things straight, and developing a better approach for life — a cycle equivalent to individual recovery.

The topic of recovery converges with the idea of pardoning, making a nuanced investigation of human connections and moral development. Pardoning, both looked for and conceded, turns into an impetus for reclamation — a scaffold between the past and a future set apart by recuperating and compromise. The demonstration of excusing oneself or others is a significant affirmation of the potential for change and the refusal to be characterized exclusively by past offenses.

In looking at the redemptive excursion, an essential perspective is the development of the person as a changed being. This change stretches out past simple social change; it envelops a significant change in one's personality, values, and comprehension of the world. The recovered individual is certainly not a simple impression of their previous slip-ups yet a recharged and re-imagined self, molded by the cauldron of reclamation.

Writing, with its capacity to enlighten the human experience, gives horde instances of characters who arise as changed people through the redemptive cycle. In Nathaniel Hawthorne's "The Red Letter," the personality of Hester Prynne goes through a redemptive excursion set apart by open disgrace, detachment, and possible acknowledgment. Hester's rise as a merciful, tough, and compassionate lady means the groundbreaking force of recovery on a singular level.

Additionally, the excursion of Frodo Baggins in J.R.R. Tolkien's "The Master of the Rings" exemplifies the subject of recovery and change. Frodo, troubled by the heaviness of the One Ring and the enticements of force, goes through massive preliminaries and difficulties. His inevitable victory over the Ring's tainting impact and the benevolent demonstration of its obliteration address Frodo's rise as a changed individual — one who has confronted the most obscure parts of himself and the world yet held his honesty.

Genuine accounts likewise swarm with instances of people who have arisen as changed creatures through the redemptive cycle. Recuperating junkies, for example, frequently talk about the significant changes they go through as they stand up to their evil presences, look for help, and modify their lives. The interaction includes going without substances as well as developing another feeling of direction, sense of pride, and a guarantee to good connections.

In the domain of law enforcement, reclamation is a subject that reverberates profoundly. The course of recovery inside remedial frameworks intends to work with the change of people who have perpetrated violations. The accentuation isn't exclusively on discipline yet on giving open doors to training, self-reflection, and expertise advancement. The objective is to empower people to reintegrate into society as changed and decent residents.

Reclamation and change are not restricted to individual accounts; they additionally track down articulation in aggregate and cultural settings. Social orders wrestling with authentic treacheries or times of moral retribution frequently go through cycles of aggregate reclamation. Truth and compromise commissions, for instance, look to recognize past wrongs, give a stage to truth-telling, and make ready for recuperating and social change.

The idea of reclamation additionally winds through the texture of mainstream society, including film. Motion pictures frequently portray characters who explore the difficult way of reclamation, facing their own imperfections and the results of their activities. In Candid Darabont's variation of Stephen Ruler's "The Shawshank Reclamation," the personality of Andy Dufresne changes the existences of everyone around him through thoughtful gestures, versatility, and an unfaltering confidence in the chance of recovery.

Music, as well, fills in as a mechanism for investigating the subject of recovery. Melodies frequently describe individual excursions of beating misfortune, looking for absolution, and embracing positive change. The verses and songs become a method for communicating the close to home scene of recovery, resounding with audience members who track down comfort, motivation, or appearance in the groundbreaking force of music.

The redemptive excursion isn't without its difficulties and intricacies. It requires a significant obligation to self-reflection, responsibility, and the burdensome undertaking of defying one's own deficiencies. The recovered individual should wrestle with the heaviness of responsibility, disgrace, and the scars of previous oversights. The interaction requests strength, boldness, and an eagerness to defy the uneasiness of confronting reality with regards to oneself.

Besides, the redemptive excursion is certainly not a straight direction however frequently includes difficulties and backslides. People might end up caught in the repetitive idea of progress, confronting the repeat of old propensities or thought designs. The vital lies in persistence and a promise to proceed with the excursion toward change, understanding that difficulties don't discredit the headway made yet are basic to the intricacy of the redemptive cycle.

The subject of rise as a changed individual envelops a significant investigation of the human limit with regards to change, development, and moral reestablishment.

This groundbreaking excursion is a typical story string tracked down in writing, religion, theory, and individual stories.

It dives into the intricacies of reclamation, self-revelation, and the development of one's personality. The rise as a changed individual addresses a key change in values, convictions, and understanding — a development that rises above past restrictions and embraces a new, illuminated self.

Writing, as an impression of the human experience, offers a rich embroidery of characters who go through the extraordinary course of rise. Exemplary works, like Fyodor Dostoevsky's "Wrongdoing and Discipline," grandstand heroes wrestling with moral predicaments and individual emergencies. Raskolnikov, the clever's focal person, goes through a significant change as he stands up to the results of his activities and encounters an ethical arousing. The rise of Raskolnikov as a changed individual represents the original's investigation of recovery, moral obligation, and the potential for self-awareness.

In J.D. Salinger's "The Catcher in the Rye," the hero, Holden Caulfield, sets out on an excursion of self-revelation and bafflement. His experiences with the grown-up world, misfortune, and individual battles add to his rise as a changed person. The novel investigates subjects of realness, distance, and the difficulties of exploring the progress from pre-adulthood to adulthood. Holden's development mirrors the all inclusive journey for personality and significance, resounding with perusers who have wrestled with the intricacies of self-revelation.

Besides, the development as a changed individual is a common subject in progress of William Shakespeare. In "Hamlet," the eponymous person goes through a significant mental change as he wrestles with distress, double-crossing, and existential inquiries. Hamlet's process reflects the intricacies of human instinct and the mission for self-understanding. The play investigates topics of vengeance, frenzy, and the groundbreaking force of thoughtfulness, finishing in Hamlet's development as a disastrous figure whose inward battles make a permanent imprint on the scholarly scene.

Strict customs likewise weave the subject of rise as a changed person into their stories. Christianity, for example, accentuates the idea of otherworldly resurrection and change. The scriptural story of Saul's transformation to turn into the messenger Paul outlines the extreme shift from a persecutor of Christians to an intense devotee and preacher. This change implies an adjustment of convictions as well as a principal shift in personality and reason — an honest development as a changed individual driven by a freshly discovered comprehension and reclamation.

In Buddhism, the possibility of edification exemplifies a definitive rise as a changed person. The verifiable Buddha, Siddhartha Gautama, went through an excursion of self-revelation, renunciation, and reflection that prompted his edification. The Buddha's lessons accentuate the potential for all people to accomplish illumination through care, moral direct, and the development of insight. The development as an edified being addresses the zenith of otherworldly change in Buddhist way of thinking.

Philosophical investigations of personality and change further add to the subject of rise as a changed person. Existentialist masterminds, for example, Jean-Paul Sartre and Albert Camus wrestle with inquiries of genuineness, opportunity, and the quest for importance. Sartre's idea of "dishonesty" highlights the significance of mindfulness and getting a sense of ownership with one's decisions — a fundamental part of the groundbreaking excursion. The existentialist point of view welcomes people to stand up to the inborn opportunity to shape their own personalities and effectively participate during the time spent becoming.

In the domain of individual accounts, people frequently share accounts of their groundbreaking processes — of conquering misfortune, exploring individual emergencies, and arising as changed creatures. These accounts feature the flexibility of the human soul and the limit with respect to development notwithstanding challenges. Whether defeating fixation, reconstructing after a misfortune, or exploring character moves, the narratives of rise as changed people resound as demonstrations of the human limit with regards to reexamination and reestablishment.

Recuperation stories inside the setting of habit offer strong instances of rise as changed people. People recuperating from substance misuse frequently go through significant changes in their mentalities, ways of behaving, and ways of life. The recuperation interaction includes self-reflection, responsibility, and the development of new survival strategies. The development as a changed person in recuperation addresses an excursion of self-revelation, mending, and the quest for a better and really satisfying life.

Moreover, the topic of rise as a changed individual reaches out into the area of brain research. The course of self-realization, as conceptualized by Abraham Maslow, lines up with the possibility of individual rise. Self-completion includes the acknowledgment of one's true capacity, the quest for self-awareness, and the capacity to rise above self inflicted restrictions. The rise as a self-completed individual addresses a comprehensive change including close to home, mental, and otherworldly aspects.

With regards to schooling, the subject of rise as a changed individual is integral to the objectives of all encompassing learning and self-improvement. Instructive encounters add to the forming of people's characters, values, and perspectives. Understudies participate in a consistent course of self-disclosure, decisive reasoning, and the development of abilities that set them up for a dynamic and interconnected world. The groundbreaking idea of schooling lies in the obtaining of information as well as in the development of people prepared to explore intricacy and contribute seriously to society.

Proficient improvement likewise lines up with the topic of rise as a changed person. As people progress in their professions, they experience difficulties, get new abilities, and go through shifts in context.

The cycle includes adjusting to evolving conditions, embracing deep rooted learning, and developing a development mentality. The development as a changed proficient mirrors a continuous obligation to greatness, versatility, and the quest for consistent improvement.

The subject of rise as a changed individual crosses with the idea of flexibility — the capacity to return from misfortune and explore life's difficulties with strength and versatility. Flexibility includes the ability to endure hardships as well as the capacity to gain from difficulties, adjust to change, and arise more grounded. The extraordinary force of strength lies during the time spent dealing with difficulty directly and involving those encounters as impetuses for self-awareness.

Genuine instances of development as changed people frequently emerge in light of cultural difficulties or snapshots of moral retribution. Developments for civil rights, for example, include people who go through an aggregate extraordinary interaction. Activists and supporters face foundational treacheries, challenge harsh designs, and work towards a more evenhanded society. The rise as changed people inside civil rights developments connotes a promise to positive change, inclusivity, and the quest for equity.

Besides, the subject of development as a changed individual is unpredictably associated with the idea of personality. Character isn't static however develops over the long run through encounters, connections, and self-reflection. The extraordinary excursion includes a renegotiation of one's character — a course of shedding old stories, embracing validness, and lining up with values that reverberate on a more profound level. The rise as a changed individual mirrors a cognizant decision to characterize oneself genuinely and to live in arrangement with one's actual qualities.

In looking at explicit models across different spaces, it becomes clear that the subject of rise as a changed individual is both widespread and various. Whether portrayed in writing, investigated in strict and philosophical customs, described in private stories, or saw in cultural developments, the extraordinary excursion addresses the common human experience of development, change, and the quest for a more significant presence.

The extraordinary excursion isn't without its difficulties, vulnerabilities, and snapshots of vagueness. It requires an eagerness to face uneasiness, explore the intricacies of self-disclosure, and embrace the vulnerabilities inborn during the time spent development. The extraordinary excursion is a persistent cycle — one that welcomes people to participate in continuous self-reflection, learning, and variation.

# Chapter 8

**The Return**

In our current reality where time streamed like a waterway, and recollections reverberated through the passages of ages, there existed a story covered in the fogs of failed to remember ages. It was a story of excursions embraced and fates weaved, of adoration that opposed the limits of presence, and of a return that held the commitment of recovery.

In the midst of the divine embroidery of the universe, there lay a planet washed in the delicate gleam of its twin moons. On this earthbound domain, a story unfurled — a story that rose above the limits of the real world and wandered into the ethereal domains of the unexplored world.

In the core of this mysterious adventure stood a hero named Eldarion, a being whose very embodiment bore the heaviness of an old prescience. The prescience discussed a return, an occasion predicted in the records of time that held the way in to the salvation of a world near the precarious edge of dimness.

Eldarion's process started in the modest town of Eldoria, settled in the hug of emerald valleys and purplish blue skies. Raised by the older folks of the town, he grew up under the generous look of the Eldertrees, old arboreal sentinels that murmured the mysteries of the universe to the people who might tune in.

From his initial years, Eldarion showed a momentous proclivity for the supernatural energies that saturated the air. The Eldertrees detected the torpid power inside him, a power that rose above the limits of the human curl. As he developed, so did his association with the natural powers that formed the actual texture of the real world.

In the quietude of Eldoria, Eldarion's tutor, a shrewd sage named Alathor, directed him on the way of self-revelation. Alathor, a manager of the old legend, discussed the Return — a grandiose occasion that would stir the torpid energies inside Eldarion and put into high gear a progression of occasions that would either proclaim the beginning of another time or dive the world into everlasting evening.

As the day of the Return moved close, Eldarion felt the flows of fate joining upon him. The heavenly bodies adjusted in a grandiose dance, and the air was pregnant with expectation. Eldoria, when a shelter of quietness, presently beat with an energy that reverberated with the pulsating heart of the universe.

Eldarion left on a journey to the Sacrosanct Woods, where the limits between the physical and otherworldly domains obscured. The Consecrated Woods, stowed away from according to the world, housed the Astral Nexus — an old conductor of grandiose energies that held the way to opening Eldarion's dormant potential.

As he entered the Forest, Eldarion felt a reverberation profound inside his spirit. The Eldertrees bowed in quiet affirmation, their leaves stirring in an extraordinary ensemble. Alathor, the revered sage, drove him to the core of the Woods, where the Astral Nexus anticipated, a throbbing nexus of brilliant energy.

With each step, Eldarion could feel the energies flowing through him, reverberating with the actual center of his being. The Astral Nexus answered his presence, its ethereal ringlets contacting interlace with his embodiment. In that radiant second, Eldarion turned into a vessel of enormous power, a channel through which the powers of creation and obliteration streamed.

As the divine energies flooded through him, Eldarion witnessed dreams of ages long past and prospects yet to unfurl. He saw developments rise and fall, wars pursued for the sake of failed to remember divine beings, and love that persevered through the assaults of time. Among the heap dreams, one stuck out — a dream of a world on the incline of destruction, where shadows took steps to immerse all that existed.

In that desperate vision, Eldarion observed a figure hung in shadows — a vindictive power that looked to obscure the illumination of creation. The figure radiated an air of perniciousness, a haziness that rose above the conventional shadows that gripped to the sides of presence. It was a harbinger of inestimable lopsidedness, a danger that could unwind the actual texture of the real world.

Still up in the air to impede the looming dimness, Eldarion arose out of the Hallowed Forest, his eyes on fire with the grandiose energies that presently flowed through his veins. The Eldertrees bowed again, their branches framing an overhang of veneration. Eldoria, detecting the change in the astronomical tides, prepared itself for the difficulties that lay ahead.

Expression of Eldarion's change spread like quickly, arriving at the farthest corners of the land. Some hailed him as the harbinger of salvation, while others saw him with anxiety, dreading the eccentric idea of enormous powers. Eldarion, troubled by the heaviness of fate, realize that his process had quite recently started.

Directed by the murmurs of the Eldertrees, Eldarion set out on a mission to look for partners despite looming murkiness. His way driven him to the itinerant clans of the Murmuring Sands, a desert domain where the breezes conveyed the privileged insights of failed to remember civilizations. Among the travelers, Eldarion experienced Sylara, a talented champion with a puzzling past.

Sylara, sensitive to the back and forth movement of the desert winds, detected the vast energies that encompassed Eldarion. A quiet comprehension passed among them, and without words, she went along with him on his journey. Together, they navigated the Murmuring Sands, looking for the insight of the antiquated soothsayers who stayed in secret desert springs.

The diviners, with eyes blurred by the cover of time, discussed a curio of heavenly beginning — the Starheart. Legend held that the Starheart was a section of a long-neglected star, permeated with the pith of creation itself. It was said to have the ability to steer the astronomical results for light or murkiness.

Eldarion and Sylara, driven by the criticalness of their mission, wandered into the profundities of the Murmuring Sands, confronting preliminaries that tried the actual center of their creatures. Dust storms murmured old enigmas, and hallucinations pulled pranks on their faculties. However, through determination and a bond produced by vast strings, they arrived at the secret desert garden where the Starheart lay lethargic.

The desert spring, washed in the gleaming light of the twin moons, supported the Starheart inside a heavenly pool. Eldarion, sensitive to the antique's reverberation, expanded his hand, and the Starheart answered, suspending over the pool. Its brilliance enlightened the desert night, creating shaded areas that moved together as one with the vast energies.

As Eldarion and Sylara wondered about the heavenly curio, a ghostly figure emerged before them. It was Aeliana, an ethereal being who had looked after the Starheart for ages. Aeliana uncovered the real essence of the curio — it was a key that could open the lethargic potential inside Eldarion, intensifying his grandiose capacities to face the infringing murkiness.

With a feeling of direction consuming in their souls, Eldarion, Sylara, and Aeliana set off to stir the idle force of the Starheart. The excursion took them to the Gem Pinnacles, a mountain range that penetrated the sky. There, in the glasslike heart of the mountains, lay the Heavenly Produce — an old manufacture said to be created by the divine beings themselves.

The Divine Fashion, washed in the iridescence of astral flares, anticipated the dash of the Starheart. Eldarion, directed by Aeliana's ethereal presence, injected the produce with the enormous energies radiating from the antique. The divine blazes thundered to life, wrapping the produce in a hypnotizing dance of creation.

As the manufacture beat with freshly discovered power, Eldarion felt the reverberation inside him strengthen. The Starheart, presently a channel of heavenly energies, converged with his pith, opening the full degree of his infinite capacities. Aeliana, her structure aglow with astral brilliance, talked about the preliminaries that looked for them — the showdown with the malicious power that tried to dive the world into everlasting evening.

Enabled by the vast implantation, Eldarion and his partners set out to go up against the shadows that lingered not too far off. The Eldertrees, their branches influencing in an enormous mourn, murmured of a get-together tempest that took steps to unwind the actual embroidery of creation. Eldoria, presently a stronghold of trust, anticipated the arrival of its extravagant child.

The malicious power, an enormous variation known as the Voidbane, had taken home in the Obsidian Bastion — a supernatural post that existed at the nexus of the real world and nothingness. The stronghold, an indication of the Void's yearning, cast a shadow that cursed the land, emptying life and light out of the world.

Eldarion, Sylara, and Aeliana, joined by a cooperation of partners drawn from various corners of the domain, moved toward the Obsidian Stronghold. The air popped with strain as they passed the boundary into a domain where the laws of physical science bowed to the impulses of the Voidbane. Reality itself appeared to twist and curve in the stronghold's damned hug.

The excursion through the stronghold's twisted corridors tried the purpose of the mates. Deceptions appeared from the most obscure openings of their psyches, and the walls murmured the questions that waited in their souls. However, directed by the vast bonds that assembled them, they, not entirely settled to stand up to the wellspring of the infringing dimness.

In the core of the Obsidian Fortress, they confronted the Voidbane — an undefined element that resisted human cognizance. Its ringlets, as inky shadows, blew up, looking to consume all that remained before it. Eldarion, presently a guide of divine power, stood up to the Voidbane with an assurance that rose above human slightness.

The fight that resulted challenged the laws of traditional fighting. Grandiose energies conflicted with the void's unyielding yearning, making an embroidery of light and shadow that painted the stronghold's walls. Sylara, her edge hitting the dance floor with ethereal effortlessness, drew in the Voidbane's signs, while Aeliana wove defensive wards to protect the friends from the deep surge.

## 8.1 The protagonist contemplates the insights gained and the impact of the journey.

In the result of the vast conflict that unfurled inside the bounds of the Obsidian Stronghold, Eldarion remained in the midst of the leftovers of the divine bedlam, his structure aglow with the waiting reverberations of astral power. The air, once pregnant with the pernicious atmosphere of the Voidbane, presently vibrated with the agreeable reverberation of grandiose balance. The scene, when defaced by the shadows of looming dimness, gave testimony regarding the groundbreaking force of heavenly resurrection.

Eldarion's look meandered across the changed landscape, his eyes mirroring the heap feelings that whirled inside his spirit. The mates who remained close by — Sylara, the hero sensitive to the murmurs of the desert winds, and Aeliana, the ethereal watchman of the Starheart — shared a quiet fellowship, their fates everlastingly weaved by the grandiose strings that had directed them through the embroidery of their excursion.

As the divine energies bit by bit died down, Eldarion wound up pondering the significant experiences acquired from the pot of his odyssey. The Eldertrees, antiquated observers to the vast show, mumbled in the delicate breeze, their leaves stirring in enormous endorsement. The Sacrosanct Woods, washed in the shiny sparkle of the twin moons, remained as a demonstration of the repetitive idea of presence and the never-ending dance among creation and disintegration.

The principal disclosure that unfolded upon Eldarion was the interconnectedness, everything being equal. Through the hardships of his excursion, he had come to figure out that each being, each animal, and each bit of stardust assumed a part in the vast ensemble. The Eldertrees, with their foundations venturing profound into the earth, exemplified this interconnected snare of life — an organization of energy that rose above the limits of individual presence.

The second understanding that pervaded Eldarion's cognizance was the fragile equilibrium that supported the universe. The vast powers, similar to the rhythmic movement of a grandiose tide, kept an unsafe harmony. The Eldertrees murmured of the everlasting battle among light and haziness, creation and destruction, and the interminable dance that guaranteed the astronomical congruity stayed solid.

As Eldarion contemplated these disclosures, his considerations went to the effect of his excursion on his general surroundings. Eldoria, when a quiet town settled in the hug of emerald valleys, had gone through a transformation. The energies released during the Return had permeated the land with an imperativeness that outperformed the unremarkable domains of mortal presence. The very air pulsated with a supernatural energy, and the Eldertrees remained as living courses of grandiose insight.

The townspeople of Eldoria, having seen the grandiose scene that unfurled before their eyes, presently lived in stunningness of the heavenly energies that penetrated their lives. Eldarion, when an unassuming occupant of the town, had turned into a figure of veneration — a living exemplification of the enormous rules that represented the universe. The Eldertrees, with their branches influencing in enormous celebration, had blessed Eldarion as the Divine Watchman, a gatekeeper entrusted with shielding the fragile balance of the world.

Following the Return, Eldarion felt a significant obligation burdening his shoulders. The enormous energies that flowed through him associated him to the actual beat of the universe. He comprehended that his job as the Divine Gatekeeper rose above the limits of individual longings or yearnings. It was a calling to act as a steward of the enormous equilibrium, to guarantee that the sensitive dance among light and dimness persevered for a long time into the future.

Sylara, the hero who had strolled close by Eldarion through the Murmuring Sands and confronted the shadows inside the Obsidian Stronghold, partook in his appearance. The desert twists, when transporters of antiquated insider facts, murmured stories of her ability and versatility. Sylara, having seen the inestimable powers that formed their predeterminations, felt a family relationship with the components — an association that went past the limits of mortal cognizance.

For Sylara, the excursion had been her very own disclosure strength and the cooperative connection between the desert winds and her fighter soul. The preliminaries inside the Murmuring Sands had improved her abilities and adjusted her to the inconspicuous harmonies of the universe. As the divine energies flooded through the Obsidian Fortress, she had hit the dance floor with the shadows, her edge slicing through the haziness with ethereal beauty.

Presently, as Sylara remained close by Eldarion following their vast victory, she considered the newly discovered reason that reverberated in the breezes. The desert, when a cruel and unforgiving span, presently bore the engravings of her excursion. The sands murmured stories of her strength, and the desert springs, unlikely treasures inside the dry scene, filled in as tokens of the desert garden where the Starheart lay torpid.

Aeliana, the ethereal watchman who had looked after the Starheart for ages, epitomized the insight of ages. Her structure, washed in astral brilliance, radiated an emanation of quietness that rose above the human loop. Aeliana, having directed Eldarion and Sylara through the Heavenly Produce and the vast cauldron of the Obsidian Fortification, took the stand concerning the back and forth movement of fates.

As Aeliana mulled over the vast disclosures, she discussed the repetitive idea of presence — the everlasting dance of creation and disintegration that formed the actual texture of the real world. The Starheart, when a lethargic section of a long-neglected star, had turned into an impetus for enormous resurrection. Aeliana, its watchman, had her impact in guaranteeing that the divine energies coursed through the veins of Eldarion, engaging him to go up against the shadows that took steps to overwhelm the world.

Together, the triplet of buddies — Eldarion, Sylara, and Aeliana — remained at the cliff of the Holy Woods, their appearance converging with the vast energies that beat through the land. The Eldertrees, quiet observers to the astronomical show, expanded their branches in enormous blessing. The world, presently washed in the delicate brilliance of the twin moons, anticipated the following part in the unfurling adventure of grandiose predetermination.

As Eldarion looked at the changed scene, he understood that the effect of their process reached out past the limits of Eldoria. The astronomical energies, presently in amicable reverberation, undulated across the domains, contacting the hearts and psyches of those receptive to the heavenly ensemble. The story of the Return, an enormous odyssey that traversed the Murmuring Sands, the Precious stone Pinnacles, and the Obsidian Fortification, resounded with creatures across the embroidery of presence.

The towns and urban communities past Eldoria demonstrated the veracity of the groundbreaking force of the infinite resurrection. Stories of Eldarion's excursion, Sylara's hit the dance floor with the shadows, and Aeliana's ethereal guardianship turned into the stuff of legends. The vast powers, ever careful, wove the strings of their story into the actual texture of folklore, guaranteeing that the reverberations of their odyssey resounded through the passages of time.

Eldarion, presently the Divine Watchman, comprehended that the effect of their process went past the substantial changes in the scene. It was a gradually expanding influence that contacted the shared perspective of the world — an update that, even with enormous vulnerabilities, the dauntless soul of trust and flexibility could shape predeterminations.

**8.2 Reintegration into the ordinary world, bringing newfound wisdom.**

As the grandiose energies settled and the reverberations of their process waited in the air, Eldarion, Sylara, and Aeliana ended up remaining at the limit of the Holy Forest. The Eldertrees, their branches influencing in vast beatitude, murmured stories of fate satisfied and the recurrent idea of presence. The world, washed in the delicate brilliance of the twin moons, anticipated the following period of their odyssey — the reintegration into the standard world.

For Eldarion, the re-visitation of Eldoria denoted the start of another section. The town, when a safe house of serenity, presently flourished as a demonstration of the extraordinary force of vast resurrection. The Eldertrees, quiet observers to the enormous show, expanded their branches in a vast salute, recognizing the Divine Watchman and his friends.

The locals of Eldoria, having seen the heavenly exhibition that unfurled before their eyes, welcomed Eldarion with a combination of stunningness and veneration. He, who had once strolled among them as a modest inhabitant, presently bore the mantle of grandiose obligation. The inestimable energies that flowed through him made him a living encapsulation of the fragile equilibrium that supported the universe.

Eldarion, playing embraced his part as the Divine Gatekeeper, tried to confer the insight acquired from his enormous excursion to the locals. In get-togethers underneath the Eldertrees, he discussed the interconnectedness of all things — the vast dance that bound each being, each animal, and each spot of stardust in an amicable embroidery of presence.

The Eldertrees, their leaves stirring in enormous endorsement, repeated Eldarion's lessons. The locals, when limited by the restrictions of mortal insight, started to figure out the inconspicuous flows of energy that coursed through the land. They figured out how to adjust themselves to the back and forth movement of the grandiose tides, tracking down comfort in the interconnected trap of life that encompassed them.

Sylara, the fighter who had confronted the shadows inside the Murmuring Sands and hit the dance floor with ethereal beauty in the core of the Obsidian Stronghold, tracked down her place in the midst of the locals. The desert twists, presently transporters of stories of her strength and ability, murmured mysteries of the astronomical dance. Sylara, once receptive to the unforgiving tunes of the desert, presently delighted in the harmonies of the interconnected universe.

She, who had crossed the dry field looking for the Starheart, presently imparted her experiences to those ready to tune in. In the twilight evenings, she remained on the hills, her outline mixing with the vast scene, and discussed the examples advanced underneath the twin moons and inside the divine manufacture. The townspeople, captivated by her stories, tracked down motivation in the dance of shadows and light that characterized their reality.

Aeliana, the ethereal watchman who had looked after the Starheart for ages, turned into a guide of serenity inside Eldoria. Her structure, washed in astral brilliance, oozed an air of serenity that pervaded the town. Aeliana, having directed Eldarion and Sylara through the inestimable pot, presently imparted her insight to the individuals who looked for comfort underneath the Eldertrees.

In calm minutes underneath the heavenly overhang, Aeliana talked about the repetitive idea of presence — the everlasting dance of creation and disintegration that formed the fates of humans. The Starheart, when a torpid part of a neglected star, had turned into an impetus for infinite resurrection. Aeliana, its watchman, filled in as a living demonstration of the persevering through nature of shrewdness that rose above the restrictions of time.

Eldarion, Sylara, and Aeliana, playing embraced their parts as stewards of grandiose equilibrium, directed the locals through the times of progress. The Eldertrees, their branches an augmentation of infinite insight, became gathering puts for conversations on the fragile dance among light and haziness. The residents, presently sensitive to the unpretentious energies that coursed through their lives, tracked down comfort in the vast rules that administered their reality.

The effect of Eldarion's process reached out past the limits of Eldoria. The infinite energies that exuded from the Return arrived at far off lands, contacting the hearts and psyches of creatures across the domains. The story of their odyssey, woven into the actual texture of folklore, turned into a wellspring of motivation for the people who looked for grasping even with enormous vulnerabilities.

Eldarion, as the Heavenly Gatekeeper, attempted ventures past the recognizable lines of Eldoria. He visited adjoining towns and urban communities, sharing the inestimable experiences acquired from the Murmuring Sands, the Gem Pinnacles, and the Obsidian Fortress. The Eldertrees, through their murmurs, directed him to where the inestimable energies were required most.

In the urban areas, where the buzzing about of mortal presence frequently darkened the enormous ensemble, Eldarion discussed the interconnectedness that bound each spirit. The natives of metropolitan scenes, encompassed by transcending structures and counterfeit lights, tracked down an association with the inestimable dance that rose above the limits of their substantial wildernesses.

Sylara, going with Eldarion on these excursions, brought the insight of the desert winds to those tucked away in the chaos of city life. She discussed the dance of shadows and light that characterized presence, empowering metropolitan inhabitants to adjust themselves to the grandiose flows that beat underneath the outer layer of their clamoring lives.

Aeliana, in her ethereal brilliance, turned into a reference point of peacefulness where the vast energies were many times muffled by the clamor of mortal desires. She visited sanctuaries and safe-havens, sharing the insight acquired from the Heavenly Produce and the infinite pot. The overseers of holy spaces, contacted by her presence, felt the unobtrusive change in the enormous energies that penetrated their consecrated grounds.

As Eldarion, Sylara, and Aeliana crossed the domains past Eldoria, they experienced creatures sensitive to the grandiose flows in their own extraordinary ways. Spiritualists, researchers, and searchers of vast bits of insight looked for direction from the threesome, perceiving in them the conveyors of heavenly experiences. The Eldertrees, through their murmurs, guided the allies to where the vast dance unfurled in mind boggling designs.

Amidst their movements, Eldarion, Sylara, and Aeliana experienced a traveling clan that had long worshipped the divine powers. The clan, existing on the edges of the Murmuring Sands, greeted the threesome wholeheartedly, perceiving in them the exemplifications of vast insight. Eldarion, in the midst of the moving rises, discussed the fragile harmony between the components and the grandiose flows that formed the desert winds.

Sylara, sensitive to the murmurs of the roaming winds, imparted her experiences to the desert-inhabitants. Together, they moved underneath the open sky, their developments an impression of the infinite dance that represented their reality. Aeliana, in her ethereal elegance, turned into a gatekeeper of the clan's hallowed ceremonies, guaranteeing that the vast energies coursed through the customs that associated them to the divine domains.

As the triplet proceeded with their excursions, they experienced old libraries that housed looks of failed to remember legend. Eldarion, encompassed by the residue of ages, dove into the infinite original copies that discussed heavenly arrangements and the inestimable cycles that molded the predeterminations of universes. Sylara, in the midst of the smelly books, revealed old predictions that repeated the murmurs of the desert winds.

Aeliana, in the consecrated corridors of information, imparted her bits of knowledge to researchers who tried to unwind the secrets of the universe. The divine energies that exuded from the friends mixed the libraries with a recharged liveliness, as though the actual pith of the infinite dance had been interpreted onto the pages of failed to remember original copies.

In each experience, Eldarion, Sylara, and Aeliana abandoned a tradition of vast insight. The effect of their process resounded in the hearts of those they experienced, winding around an embroidery of grasping that rose above the restrictions of mortal discernment. The Eldertrees, through their murmurs, conveyed a vast beatitude, recognizing the significant effect of their odyssey.

As Eldarion, Sylara, and Aeliana crossed the domains, they found pockets of haziness that actually stuck to the enormous embroidery. Vindictive powers, remainders of the Voidbane's impact, looked to upset the fragile equilibrium that the triplet had endeavored to reestablish. The Eldertrees, through their murmurs, made the friends aware of the waiting shadows that took steps to inundate specific domains.

Eldarion, perceiving the obligation that accompanied his job as the Divine Gatekeeper, dealt with these difficulties directly. The vast energies that flowed through him turned into a signal of light notwithstanding infringing dimness. Sylara, her cutting edge hitting the dance floor with ethereal effortlessness, went up against the shadows that tried to oppose the grandiose balance. Aeliana, in her ethereal brilliance, wove defensive wards to protect the domains from the pernicious powers that tried to disentangle the fragile dance among light and murkiness.

Amidst these grandiose showdowns, the triplet found curios of divine beginning — relics permeated with the pith of the enormous powers. Eldarion, directed by the murmurs of the Eldertrees, opened the dormant power inside these curios, utilizing them to expel the shadows that waited in the secret corners of the domains.

The effect of these experiences resonated across the universe, sending swells through the interconnected trap of presence. The Eldertrees, their branches reaching out into the vast flows, recognized the buddies' endeavors in protecting the sensitive equilibrium that supported the universe.

As Eldarion, Sylara, and Aeliana ventured through the domains, they experienced a general public of divine researchers who had devoted their lives to disentangling the secrets of the universe. The researchers, perceiving in the triplet the living exemplifications of enormous insight

**8.3 Reflection on personal growth and the significance of the discoveries.**

As the grandiose energies settled and the reverberations of their process waited in the air, Eldarion, Sylara, and Aeliana ended up remaining at the limit of the Holy Forest. The Eldertrees, their branches influencing in vast beatitude, murmured stories of fate satisfied and the recurrent idea of presence. The world, washed in the delicate brilliance of the twin moons, anticipated the following period of their odyssey — the reintegration into the standard world.

For Eldarion, the re-visitation of Eldoria denoted the start of another section. The town, when a safe house of serenity, presently flourished as a demonstration of the extraordinary force of vast resurrection. The Eldertrees, quiet observers to the enormous show, expanded their branches in a vast salute, recognizing the Divine Watchman and his friends.

The locals of Eldoria, having seen the heavenly exhibition that unfurled before their eyes, welcomed Eldarion with a combination of stunningness and veneration.

He, who had once strolled among them as a modest inhabitant, presently bore the mantle of grandiose obligation. The inestimable energies that flowed through him made him a living encapsulation of the fragile equilibrium that supported the universe.

Eldarion, playing embraced his part as the Divine Gatekeeper, tried to confer the insight acquired from his enormous excursion to the locals. In get-togethers underneath the Eldertrees, he discussed the interconnectedness of all things — the vast dance that bound each being, each animal, and each spot of stardust in an amicable embroidery of presence.

The Eldertrees, their leaves stirring in enormous endorsement, repeated Eldarion's lessons. The locals, when limited by the restrictions of mortal insight, started to figure out the inconspicuous flows of energy that coursed through the land. They figured out how to adjust themselves to the back and forth movement of the grandiose tides, tracking down comfort in the interconnected trap of life that encompassed them.

Sylara, the fighter who had confronted the shadows inside the Murmuring Sands and hit the dance floor with ethereal beauty in the core of the Obsidian Stronghold, tracked down her place in the midst of the locals. The desert twists, presently transporters of stories of her strength and ability, murmured mysteries of the astronomical dance. Sylara, once receptive to the unforgiving tunes of the desert, presently delighted in the harmonies of the interconnected universe.

She, who had crossed the dry field looking for the Starheart, presently imparted her experiences to those ready to tune in. In the twilight evenings, she remained on the hills, her outline mixing with the vast scene, and discussed the examples advanced underneath the twin moons and inside the divine manufacture. The townspeople, captivated by her stories, tracked down motivation in the dance of shadows and light that characterized their reality.

Aeliana, the ethereal watchman who had looked after the Starheart for ages, turned into a guide of serenity inside Eldoria. Her structure, washed in astral brilliance, oozed an air of serenity that pervaded the town. Aeliana, having directed Eldarion and Sylara through the inestimable pot, presently imparted her insight to the individuals who looked for comfort underneath the Eldertrees.

In calm minutes underneath the heavenly overhang, Aeliana talked about the repetitive idea of presence — the everlasting dance of creation and disintegration that formed the fates of humans. The Starheart, when a torpid part of a neglected star, had turned into an impetus for infinite resurrection. Aeliana, its watchman, filled in as a living demonstration of the persevering through nature of shrewdness that rose above the restrictions of time.

Eldarion, Sylara, and Aeliana, playing embraced their parts as stewards of grandiose equilibrium, directed the locals through the times of progress. The Eldertrees, their branches an augmentation of infinite insight, became gathering puts for conversations on the fragile dance among light and haziness. The residents, presently sensitive to the unpretentious energies that coursed through their lives, tracked down comfort in the vast rules that administered their reality.

The effect of Eldarion's process reached out past the limits of Eldoria. The infinite energies that exuded from the Return arrived at far off lands, contacting the hearts and psyches of creatures across the domains. The story of their odyssey, woven into the actual texture of folklore, turned into a wellspring of motivation for the people who looked for grasping even with enormous vulnerabilities.

Eldarion, as the Heavenly Gatekeeper, attempted ventures past the recognizable lines of Eldoria. He visited adjoining towns and urban communities, sharing the inestimable experiences acquired from the Murmuring Sands, the Gem Pinnacles, and the Obsidian Fortress. The Eldertrees, through their murmurs, directed him to where the inestimable energies were required most.

In the urban areas, where the buzzing about of mortal presence frequently darkened the enormous ensemble, Eldarion discussed the interconnectedness that bound each spirit. The natives of metropolitan scenes, encompassed by transcending structures and counterfeit lights, tracked down an association with the inestimable dance that rose above the limits of their substantial wildernesses.

Sylara, going with Eldarion on these excursions, brought the insight of the desert winds to those tucked away in the chaos of city life. She discussed the dance of shadows and light that characterized presence, empowering metropolitan inhabitants to adjust themselves to the grandiose flows that beat underneath the outer layer of their clamoring lives.

Aeliana, in her ethereal brilliance, turned into a reference point of peacefulness where the vast energies were many times muffled by the clamor of mortal desires. She visited sanctuaries and safe-havens, sharing the insight acquired from the Heavenly Produce and the infinite pot. The overseers of holy spaces, contacted by her presence, felt the unobtrusive change in the enormous energies that penetrated their consecrated grounds.

As Eldarion, Sylara, and Aeliana crossed the domains past Eldoria, they experienced creatures sensitive to the grandiose flows in their own extraordinary ways. Spiritualists, researchers, and searchers of vast bits of insight looked for direction from the threesome, perceiving in them the conveyors of heavenly experiences. The Eldertrees, through their murmurs, guided the allies to where the vast dance unfurled in mind boggling designs.

Amidst their movements, Eldarion, Sylara, and Aeliana experienced a traveling clan that had long worshipped the divine powers. The clan, existing on the edges of the Murmuring Sands, greeted the threesome wholeheartedly, perceiving in them the exemplifications of vast insight. Eldarion, in the midst of the moving rises, discussed the fragile harmony between the components and the grandiose flows that formed the desert winds.

Sylara, sensitive to the murmurs of the roaming winds, imparted her experiences to the desert-inhabitants. Together, they moved underneath the open sky, their developments an impression of the infinite dance that represented their reality. Aeliana, in her ethereal elegance, turned into a gatekeeper of the clan's hallowed ceremonies, guaranteeing that the vast energies coursed through the customs that associated them to the divine domains.

As the triplet proceeded with their excursions, they experienced old libraries that housed looks of failed to remember legend. Eldarion, encompassed by the residue of ages, dove into the infinite original copies that discussed heavenly arrangements and the inestimable cycles that molded the predeterminations of universes. Sylara, in the midst of the smelly books, revealed old predictions that repeated the murmurs of the desert winds.

Aeliana, in the consecrated corridors of information, imparted her bits of knowledge to researchers who tried to unwind the secrets of the universe. The divine energies that exuded from the friends mixed the libraries with a recharged liveliness, as though the actual pith of the infinite dance had been interpreted onto the pages of failed to remember original copies.

In each experience, Eldarion, Sylara, and Aeliana abandoned a tradition of vast insight. The effect of their process resounded in the hearts of those they experienced, winding around an embroidery of grasping that rose above the restrictions of mortal discernment. The Eldertrees, through their murmurs, conveyed a vast beatitude, recognizing the significant effect of their odyssey.

As Eldarion, Sylara, and Aeliana crossed the domains, they found pockets of haziness that actually stuck to the enormous embroidery. Vindictive powers, remainders of the Voidbane's impact, looked to upset the fragile equilibrium that the triplet had endeavored to reestablish. The Eldertrees, through their murmurs, made the friends aware of the waiting shadows that took steps to inundate specific domains.

Eldarion, perceiving the obligation that accompanied his job as the Divine Gatekeeper, dealt with these difficulties directly. The vast energies that flowed through him turned into a signal of light notwithstanding infringing dimness. Sylara, her cutting edge hitting the dance floor with ethereal effortlessness, went up against the shadows that tried to oppose the grandiose balance. Aeliana, in her ethereal brilliance, wove defensive wards to protect the domains from the pernicious powers that tried to disentangle the fragile dance among light and murkiness.

Amidst these grandiose showdowns, the triplet found curios of divine beginning — relics permeated with the pith of the enormous powers. Eldarion, directed by the murmurs of the Eldertrees, opened the dormant power inside these curios, utilizing them to expel the shadows that waited in the secret corners of the domains.

The effect of these experiences resonated across the universe, sending swells through the interconnected trap of presence. The Eldertrees, their branches reaching out into the vast flows, recognized the buddies' endeavors in protecting the sensitive equilibrium that supported the universe.

As Eldarion, Sylara, and Aeliana ventured through the domains, they experienced a general public of divine researchers who had devoted their lives to disentangling the secrets of the universe. The researchers, perceiving in the triplet the living exemplifications of enormous insight

In the cities, where the hustle and bustle often obscured the cosmic symphony, Eldarion spoke of the interconnectedness of personal growth with the delicate balance between light and darkness. Sylara, her silhouette blending with the urban landscape, shared her insights into the dance of shadows and light that defined existence. Aeliana, in her ethereal radiance, became a source of serenity in places where the cosmic energies were often drowned out by the noise of mortal ambitions.

The companions, guided by the whispers of the Eldertrees, encountered beings across the realms who sought understanding in the face of cosmic uncertainties. Eldarion, Sylara, and Aeliana, through their cosmic reflections, became beacons of hope for those navigating the intricacies of personal growth. The Eldertrees, extending their branches in cosmic benediction, conveyed approval for the companions' efforts in sharing the significance of their discoveries.

In the midst of their travels, Eldarion, Sylara, and Aeliana encountered a nomadic tribe that had long revered the celestial forces.

The tribe, existing on the fringes of the Whispering Sands, welcomed the trio with open arms, recognizing in them the living embodiments of cosmic wisdom. Eldarion, amidst the shifting dunes, spoke of the interconnectedness of personal growth with the dance of the desert winds.

Sylara, attuned to the whispers of the nomadic winds, shared her insights with the desert-dwellers. Together, they danced beneath the open sky, their movements a reflection of the cosmic dance that governed their existence. Aeliana, in her ethereal grace, became a guardian of the tribe's sacred rites, ensuring that the cosmic energies flowed through the rituals that connected them to the celestial realms.

The impact of their encounters with different societies and beings resonated with the trio. The Eldertrees, through their whispers, conveyed the universality of personal growth and the cosmic dance that transcended cultural and geographical boundaries. Eldarion, Sylara, and Aeliana, as emissaries of cosmic wisdom, recognized the significance of their journey in fostering understanding among beings across the tapestry of existence.

As the trio continued their travels, they encountered ancient libraries that housed scrolls of forgotten lore. Eldarion, surrounded by the dust of ages, delved into the cosmic manuscripts that spoke of celestial alignments and the cosmic cycles that shaped the destinies of worlds. Sylara, amidst the musty tomes, uncovered ancient prophecies that echoed the whispers of the desert winds.

Aeliana, in the hallowed halls of knowledge, shared her insights with scholars who sought to unravel the mysteries of the cosmos. The Eldertrees, through their whispers, conveyed approval for the collaboration between the companions and the seekers of celestial truths. The cosmic energies that emanated from the companions infused the libraries with a renewed vibrancy, as if the very essence of the cosmic dance had been transcribed onto the pages of forgotten manuscripts.

In each encounter, Eldarion, Sylara, and Aeliana left behind a legacy of cosmic wisdom. The impact of their journey resonated in the hearts of those they encountered, weaving a tapestry of understanding that transcended the limitations of mortal perception. The Eldertrees, through their whispers, conveyed a cosmic benediction, acknowledging the profound impact of their odyssey.

As Eldarion, Sylara, and Aeliana traversed the realms, they discovered pockets of darkness that still clung to the cosmic tapestry. Malevolent forces, remnants of the Voidbane's influence, sought to disrupt the delicate balance that the trio had worked so hard to restore. The Eldertrees, through their whispers, alerted the companions to the lingering shadows that threatened to engulf certain realms.

Eldarion, recognizing the responsibility that came with his role as the Celestial Guardian, faced these challenges head-on. The cosmic energies that coursed through him became a beacon of light in the face of encroaching darkness. Sylara, her blade dancing with ethereal grace, confronted the shadows that sought to defy the cosmic equilibrium. Aeliana, in her ethereal radiance, wove protective wards to shield the realms from the malevolent forces that sought to unravel the delicate dance between light and darkness.

In the midst of these cosmic confrontations, the trio discovered artifacts of celestial origin—relics imbued with the essence of the cosmic forces. Eldarion, guided by the whispers of the Eldertrees, unlocked the latent power within these artifacts, using them to banish the shadows that lingered in the hidden corners of the realms.

The impact of these encounters reverberated across the cosmos, sending ripples through the interconnected web of existence. The Eldertrees, their branches extending into the cosmic currents, acknowledged the companions' efforts in preserving the delicate balance that sustained the universe.

As Eldarion, Sylara, and Aeliana journeyed through the realms, they encountered a society of celestial scholars who had dedicated their lives to unraveling the mysteries of the cosmos. The scholars, recognizing in the trio the living embodiments of cosmic wisdom, welcomed them into their sanctuaries of knowledge.

Eldarion, amidst the celestial scrolls and star maps, exchanged insights with the scholars who delved into the cosmic forces that governed the heavens. Sylara, surrounded by celestial charts and diagrams, shared her understanding of the dance between the stars and the desert winds. Aeliana, in her ethereal grace, became a muse for the celestial scholars, inspiring new avenues of cosmic exploration.

The Eldertrees, through their whispers, conveyed approval for the collaboration between the companions and the celestial scholars. The cosmic energies that pulsed through the sanctuaries of knowledge resonated with the harmonious dance of enlightenment, creating

# Chapter 9

**The Ever-Unfolding Journey**

The excursion of life is a confounded embroidery woven with the strings of time, insight, and the consistently present vulnerability representing things to come. Every individual leaves on a remarkable odyssey, an individual story that unfurls slowly, uncovering both the significant and the ordinary. The Steadily Unfurling Excursion is a demonstration of the human soul's flexibility, versatility, and resolute quest for importance in a world portrayed by consistent change.

As we navigate the scenes of our reality, we experience heap difficulties and wins that shape the forms of our personality. From the guiltlessness of life as a youngster to the intricacies of adulthood, the excursion is a continuum of self-revelation. The early parts of life are frequently painted with the energetic tints of interest and vast creative mind. In the jungle gyms of youth, chuckling reverberates, kinships blossom, and the world is a material ready to be painted with the brushstrokes of vast conceivable outcomes.

However, even in the untainted long stretches of youth, shadows cast by the unavoidable ghost of progress start to extend. The change from immaturity to adulthood is a pot where the liquid metal of dreams and yearnings is produced into the solid composite of obligation. The quest for information turns into a signal directing us through the maze of decisions that characterize our direction. Schooling, a foundation of self-improvement, outfits us with the devices to explore the intricacies of a steadily developing world.

The scholastic halls, whether fixed with ivy or reverberating with the hurrying around of metropolitan life, become cauldrons of change. Here, the psyche is sharpened, viewpoints widened, and deep rooted bonds fashioned. It is a phase where the seeds of enthusiasm are planted, developing into the trees that will bear the products of a deliberate presence. The excursion through scholarly community isn't simply a gathering of statistical data points; it is a transformation of the keenness and soul.

As the pages of our own stories turn, we end up remaining at the junction of decision. The choices made in these urgent minutes resound through the halls of time, forming the shapes of our fate. Profession ways unfurl like unseen paths, enticing us to investigate the strange regions of our true capacity. The expert excursion, an equal story entwining with the individual, is a demonstration of the flexibility of the human will notwithstanding difficulties.

In the kaleidoscope of callings, every job is a special shade adding to the mosaic of society. From the white-covered healers in the blessed corridors of medication to the draftsmen molding horizons, from the craftsmen whose manifestations embellish walls to the researchers examining the secrets of the universe, the range of callings is all around as different as the human experience itself. The quest for greatness turns into a compass, directing us through the wandering ways of profession development and self-realization.

However, the excursion isn't without its portion of tempests. Snags, misfortunes, and disappointments cast their shadows, testing the grit of the human soul. It is at these times of misfortune that versatility arises as a quiet yet intense sidekick. The capacity to climate the whirlwinds, gain from disappointments, and arise more grounded characterizes the genuine quintessence of the steadily unfurling venture.

In the domain of connections, the embroidery of life is woven with the sensitive strings of human associations. Family, companions, better halves — every relationship adds its extraordinary surface to the story. The familial bonds, frequently the bedrock of everyday encouragement, are the primary strings woven into the texture of our lives. The chuckling around the supper table, the common tears during snapshots of distress, and the implicit comprehension that rises above words — all add to the rich mosaic of family ties.

Companionships, those fortunate experiences that bloom into significant associations, are the beautiful strings that bungle the embroidered artwork. Companions become the mainstays of help, the associates with whom we share the victories and afflictions of life. The excellence of companionship lies in its capacity to rise above existence, staying enduring even as the excursion takes us to far off shores.

Heartfelt connections, energetic and wild, add their own shades to the material. Love, with its horde articulations, becomes both a wellspring of significant delight and a cauldron of weakness. The exchange of feelings, the dance of closeness, and the common dreams manufacture a bond that meshes two predeterminations into a solitary, mind boggling design.

However, similar to any woven artwork, connections are helpless to the mileage of time. The strings might shred, and the tones might blur, yet the recollections wait as permanent engravings on the texture of the heart. The capacity to explore the intricacies of human association, to pardon and be excused, is a fundamental piece of the always unfurling venture.

In the amazing auditorium of life, where connections become the overwhelming focus, oneself expects the job of both hero and chief. Self-disclosure turns into the directing light, enlightening the way to validness. The mission to grasp one's qualities, convictions, and goals is an excursion of contemplation that rises above the shallow layers of character.

The outer features of accomplishment might sparkle, however the inside scene characterizes the wealth of the excursion. The quest for mindfulness is certainly not a lone undertaking; it is a discourse with the internal identity, an investigation of the profundities that lie underneath the surface. Through thoughtfulness, we unearth the lost fortunes of strength, sympathy, and compassion that improve the human experience.

As we explore the maze of oneself, we experience the shadows of uncertainty and instability. The cultural assumptions, the correlation with others, and the constant quest for a tricky flawlessness cast their long shadows. It is at these times of weakness that the excursion turns into a mission for self-acknowledgment — a journey to embrace the defective, the imperfect, and the flawlessly human self.

The consistently unfurling venture is definitely not a straight story; it is an embroidery woven with the strings of development and change. Each stage, set apart by its interesting difficulties and disclosures, adds to the mosaic of an everyday routine very much experienced. The certainty of progress, the steady transition of conditions, pushes the story forward, asking us to adjust, develop, and embrace the unexplored world.

In the domain of feelings, satisfaction and distress dance pair, each supplementing the other. The ensemble of satisfaction, with its chipper notes, resounds at the times of win, achievement, and association.

A tune elevates the soul, implanting the excursion with a feeling of direction and satisfaction. However, bliss, similar to a passing tune, is transient, and the reverberations of satisfaction blend with the quietness of isolation.

Distress, with its grave harmonies, adds profundity to the piece of life. Misfortune, deplorability, and disillusionment are the piercing notes that accentuate the excursion, leaving permanent engravings on the spirit. It is in the pot of distress that versatility is tried, and the human soul arises, tempered and fortified by the flares of difficulty.

The profound scene is likewise set apart by the tints of enthusiasm and reason. The quest for energy, whether in the domains of workmanship, science, or compassionate undertakings, mixes the excursion with a feeling of imperativeness. The fire consumes in the heart, driving us forward with faithful assurance. Reason, the North Star that directs the excursion, changes the commonplace into the unprecedented, mixing each activity with importance.

### 9.1 The conclusion reflects on the ongoing nature of discovery.

Consistently unfurling and dynamic, the excursion of life is a nonstop investigation of self, others, and the unfathomable domains of presence. As we cross the unpredictable pathways of our singular stories, the strings of involvement, development, and versatility weave an embroidery that is both perplexing and consistently developing. The finish of this continuous odyssey coaxes reflection on the idea of revelation — of oneself, the world, and the interconnectedness that characterizes the human experience.

In the embroidery of life, the journey for self-disclosure stays an enduring string, entwining with each feature of our reality. The excursion inside, an overly complex investigation of the internal scene, is a journey toward grasping the profundities of our personality. An excursion rises above the shallow layers, digging into the guiding principle, convictions, and yearnings that characterize what our identity is.

The continuous exchange with oneself is definitely not a straight movement however a recurrent dance of contemplation, mindfulness, and self-acknowledgment. The mirror held up to the spirit mirrors the consistently moving forms of personality, molded by experience, development, and the pot of difficulties. The finish of this internal excursion is definitely not a proper objective however a persistent disclosure, an affirmation that oneself is a unique embroidery of logical inconsistencies, intricacies, and expected ready to be released.

As we explore the outer scenes of our lives, the always unfurling venture converges with the cultural account. Society, a complicated embroidery woven with the strings of culture, standards, and aggregate desires, becomes both the setting and the stage for our singular stories. The transaction between the individual and the cultural, the microcosm and the cosmos, shapes the forms of our excursion in manners both unpretentious and significant.

The cultural story, set apart by its own development, difficulties, and wins, turns into a mirror mirroring the aggregate ethos of a local area, a country, or humankind in general. The end drawn from this multifacetedness is that our singular processes are not detached however complicatedly associated with the more extensive flows of cultural change. The acknowledgment of this relationship requires a nuanced comprehension of our jobs as people in adding to the steadily developing story of society.

Chasing information, one more imperative string in the embroidery of revelation, the determination is definitely not a static endpoint yet an affirmation of the tremendous span that stays neglected. Information, a reference point directing the excursion, is both a wellspring of light and a sign of the boundless boondocks that call. The continuous mission for information drives us to push limits, question suppositions, and look for grasping even with intricacy.

The domains of science, craftsmanship, reasoning, and bunch different disciplines become the scenes where revelation unfurls. The end drawn from these scholarly undertakings is that the quest for information is certainly not a lone undertaking however an aggregate endeavor that rises above individual limits. The cooperative idea of disclosure, the sharing of bits of knowledge, and the union of assorted points of view add to the extravagance of the human scholarly woven artwork.

In the expert circle, where the strings of profession and employment are woven, the end is that the excursion is certainly not a direct trip however a progression of pinnacles and valleys. The quest for greatness, the improving of abilities, and the route of vocation decisions are indispensable parts of the expert odyssey. The end drawn from this space is that achievement is a unique idea, formed by self-awareness, versatility, and the capacity to adjust to the consistently changing requests of the expert scene.

The expert excursion additionally converges with the more extensive story of cultural advancement. The effect of one's livelihood on the aggregate prosperity, the commitment to local area advancement, and the moral contemplations in proficient decisions become strings in the bigger woven artwork of cultural development. The determination is that a significant expert excursion is one that adjusts individual desires to a more extensive feeling of direction, adding to the improvement of both individual lives and the aggregate human experience.

Connections, those complex strings that wind through the texture of life, likewise lead to an end that is both delicate and significant. The end drawn from the embroidery of connections is that association is the quintessence of the human experience. The delights of shared minutes, the strength got from common help, and the versatility developed through relational bonds become fundamental to the consistently unfurling venture.

However, the end additionally recognizes the delicacy of connections, the unavoidable back and forth movement of associations, and the temporariness that shadows even the most significant human bonds. It is in the acknowledgment of this fleetingness that the decision turns into a call for presence, appreciation, and the supporting of associations right now.

Feeling, with its horde articulations, adds tone and profundity to the embroidery of life. The end drawn from the close to home scene is that the human experience is an ensemble of bliss and distress, energy and reason. The capacity to explore the nuanced exchange of feelings, to enjoy the experiences of joy, and to find flexibility despite difficulty is a demonstration of the wealth of the consistently unfurling venture.

The finish of the close to home account isn't a departure from torment yet an affirmation that weakness is the pot where strength is produced. It is in the affirmation of our common humankind, with its weaknesses and blemishes, that sympathy, empathy, and a profound feeling of association arise.

In the fantastic performance center of life, the always unfurling venture is additionally set apart by the repetitive idea of seasons. The end drawn from the woven artwork of time is that change isn't simply unavoidable however characteristic for the actual idea of presence. The times of life — youth, adulthood, development — carry with them unmistakable encounters, difficulties, and amazing open doors for development.

The determination isn't a longing for a static, constant presence yet an acknowledgment of the recurring pattern, the patterns of creation and disintegration that portray the enormous dance of life. The insight got from the end is that embracing the consistently changing nature of presence considers a more liquid, versatile commitment with the excursion.

As we stand at the edge of the end, looking at the complex embroidery of our lives, the strings of revelation keep on winding around their examples. The end isn't an endpoint however a delay — a second to reflect, incorporate, and assemble strength for the sections yet to unfurl. The excursion, with its heap exciting bends in the road, is a consistently unfurling story, and the determination is nevertheless an accentuation mark in the ceaseless progression of time.

In the quiet between breaths, in the tranquility between minutes, the decision turns into a thoughtful space where appreciation for the excursion, with every one of its intricacies and wonders, arises. Appreciation for the chuckling that reverberated in the halls of happiness, appreciation for the tears that scrubbed the injuries of the spirit, and appreciation for the versatility that considered development notwithstanding challenges.

The end, in its pith, is a festival of the excursion — the embroidery of revelation that is both extraordinary and generally human. It is a challenge to keep investigating, learning, and embracing the consistently unfurling nature of presence.

The strings of disclosure, similar to waterways coursing through the scene of life, convey with them the commitment of new skylines, more profound comprehension, and the excellence innate in the actual excursion.

**9.2 The protagonist realizes that the journey never truly ends.**

In the great embroidery of presence, the acknowledgment first lights upon the hero that the excursion is a continuum, a never-ending investigation of self, connections, information, and the consistently moving scenes of life. A revelation rises above the limits of existence, reverberating through the halls of the hero's awareness. This disclosure turns into a core value, a comprehension that the odyssey isn't restricted to a particular time period or a bunch of foreordained sections however a continuous story that unfurls with every breath, every heartbeat.

The hero's consciousness of the ceaseless idea of the excursion isn't a wellspring of exhaustion however a wellspring of motivation. It is an affirmation that development isn't an objective yet a unique interaction — an excursion inside the excursion. The individual development, set apart by self-revelation, flexibility, and the constant quest for significance, turns into the hero's compass, guiding through the intricacies of life.

In the domain of connections, this acknowledgment takes on significant importance. The strings of association, woven into the texture of the hero's life, are not static however unique, ceaselessly developing. The end drawn is that connections are not limited sections with conveniently characterized starting points and endings yet authentic substances that develop, change, and adjust close by the people in question.

The hero thinks about the different connections — family, companions, better halves — and perceives that the profundity and surface of these associations change after some time. The bonds framed in the pot of shared encounters, chuckling, and tears are versatile, fit for facing the hardships of life. The acknowledgment that connections are an essential piece of the consistently unfurling venture drives the hero to move toward them with a feeling of presence, appreciation, and the comprehension that they are a continuous story as opposed to a decent objective.

The excursion of self-disclosure, a steadily extending undertaking into the internal domains, turns into a focal topic in the hero's acknowledgment. The end drawn is that oneself is certainly not a static substance yet a dynamic, multi-layered being with layers ready to be stripped back. The hero perceives that each experience, whether victorious or testing, adds to the molding of oneself. In the pot of mindfulness, the hero tracks down the mental fortitude to face weaknesses, embrace flaws, and develop a more profound comprehension of individual qualities and goals.

The continuous idea of the excursion inside turns into a wellspring of strengthening for the hero. It is a comprehension that self-improvement isn't restricted to explicit achievements yet an unfurling cycle that goes with the person through different phases of life. The acknowledgment that oneself is a material, ready to be painted with the brushstrokes of strength, empathy, and legitimacy, moves the hero forward with a feeling of direction and interest.

Information, a directing light in the consistently unfurling venture, turns into a domain where the hero finds the excellence of scholarly investigation. The end is that the quest for information is unfathomable, a mission that rises above the imperatives of reality. The hero perceives that the delight of disclosure lies in the obtaining of realities as well as in the vast conceivable outcomes that information opens up.

The investigation of different disciplines — science, workmanship, reasoning — turns into a journey of the psyche, a continuous undertaking to disentangle the secrets of the universe. The acknowledgment that the excursion of information is an undertaking without a last objective urges the hero to move toward learning with a feeling of miracle, lowliness, and the mindfulness that every revelation is a venturing stone to a more profound comprehension of the tremendous embroidery of human information.

The expert excursion, set apart by difficulties, victories, and nonstop development, adjusts consistently with the hero's acknowledgment of the ceaseless idea of the odyssey. The decision made is that a vocation is definitely not a static direction yet a powerful way with potential open doors for reexamination, investigation, and the quest for significant commitments. The hero embraces that proficient satisfaction isn't bound to accomplishing predefined objectives however is a nonstop course of development, transformation, and the arrangement of individual qualities with professional pursuits.

The cultural account, an always advancing setting to the hero's excursion, is likewise impacted by the acknowledgment that change is consistent. The end drawn is that cultural standards, values, and assumptions are liquid, dependent upon change after some time. The hero perceives the interconnectedness between private decisions and cultural advancement, understanding that singular activities add to the aggregate account of mankind.

The consciousness of the continuous idea of the excursion prompts the hero to draw in with cultural difficulties and valuable open doors with a feeling of obligation. The acknowledgment that each individual is a member in the co-making of the cultural embroidery urges the hero to contribute decidedly, cultivating sympathy, empathy, and a guarantee to social advancement.

Embracing the steadily unfurling nature of the excursion, the hero tracks down comfort in the profound scene. The end is that feelings, with their rhythmic movement, add profundity and variety to the woven artwork of life.

The hero figures out that satisfaction, distress, love, and enthusiasm are not segregated encounters but rather interconnected strings that wind through the unpredictable texture of the human experience.

The acknowledgment that weakness isn't a shortcoming however a wellspring of solidarity changes the hero's relationship with feelings. The end drawn is that close to home flexibility, developed through an acknowledgment of the nuanced interaction of sentiments, is a useful asset for exploring the difficulties of the consistently unfurling venture.

As the hero remains at the intersection of the past, present, and future, the acknowledgment flourishes that the excursion never genuinely closes — it just changes. The decision made isn't a regret for an inaccessible objective however a festival of the ceaseless movement innate throughout everyday life. The hero comprehends that every second is a take-off point for the following experience, each experience a venturing stone in the development of oneself.

The continuous idea of the excursion turns into a wellspring of freedom for the hero. It is an encouragement to live completely in the present, to appreciate the lavishness of every second, and to move toward the obscure with interest as opposed to fear. The acknowledgment that the excursion is a gift, with its vulnerabilities, challenges, and delights, encourages a feeling of appreciation and a profound appreciation for the excellence intrinsic in the steadily unfurling story of life.

In the calm snapshots of reflection, the hero thinks about the embroidered artwork woven by the strings of involvement, connections, information, and self-disclosure. The determination isn't an irrevocability yet a respite — a breath before the following breathe in, a snapshot of tranquility before the subsequent stage. The hero conveys forward the examples, strength, and astuteness acquired from the continuous excursion, realizing that the experience proceeds, and each page turned is an encouragement to find again. The acknowledgment turns into a mantra, reverberating in the offices of the heart: the excursion never genuinely closes; it just changes, develops, and unfurls with each first light of another day.

### 9.3 Open-ended possibilities for future adventures and explorations.

In the tremendous breadth of the steadily unfurling venture, the hero remains at the junction of plausibility, looking into the distance where unassuming undertakings and investigations call. The acknowledgment that the odyssey isn't restricted to a foreordained content however is an improvisational hit the dance floor with unassuming potential outcomes turns into a wellspring of elation and expectation. The excursion, as opposed to a direct direction, unfurls like a maze with neglected ways, stowed away chambers, and the commitment of disclosure every step of the way.

The unconditional idea representing things to come turns into a material ready to be painted with the brushstrokes of dreams, desires, and the vast capability of the human soul. The hero, powered by a feeling of interest and the excitement of the obscure, embraces that the excursion isn't an objective however a persistent unfurling story — a story with sections yet to be composed.

In the domain of self-revelation, the unassuming prospects become an encouragement to dive further into the layers of personality. The hero perceives that oneself is a dynamic, developing substance with the limit with respect to persistent development and change. The end drawn is that the investigation of oneself is a continuous journey, an excursion inside the excursion, where every disclosure turns into a venturing stone to new components of understanding.

The receptiveness to self-revelation likewise includes a readiness to stand up to vulnerabilities and embrace the intricacies inborn in self-improvement. The hero, as opposed to looking for a proper character, revels in the smoothness of oneself, permitting the developing story to naturally unfurl. It is an affirmation that the excursion inside is an undertaking with astonishments, challenges, and the potential for self-reexamination.

In the domain of connections, the unassuming prospects manifest as an affirmation that the associations fashioned are not static yet unique, fit for developing and extending over the long haul. The hero approaches associations with a receptiveness to new associations, different viewpoints, and the acknowledgment that each experience holds the possibility to improve the embroidered artwork of life.

The investigation of connections reaches out past the natural, welcoming the hero to develop associations that rise above social, geological, and cultural limits. The end drawn is that the receptiveness to different connections expands the range of human experience, cultivating sympathy, understanding, and a feeling of shared mankind.

Close connections, specifically, become a domain of investigation where the unassuming idea of affection unfurls like a sensitive bloom. The hero embraces that adoration isn't restricted to a solitary, foreordained story yet is a no nonsense element that adjusts, develops, and winds around its own extraordinary story. The unconditional potential outcomes in close connections become a wellspring of fervor, energy, and the delight of co-making a story that is remarkably the hero's own.

The unconditional investigation of information turns into a deep rooted mission, with the hero as a ceaseless searcher of shrewdness and understanding. The acknowledgment that the quest for information realizes no limits moves the hero into assorted domains of request — science, expressions, reasoning, and then some.

The unassuming prospects chasing information become a wellspring of motivation, empowering the hero to address, challenge, and embrace the strange domains of scholarly investigation.

The scholar and scholarly pursuits become not just a necessary evil but rather an excursion of persistent revelation. The hero, directed by an unquenchable interest, looks for information not for gathering but rather as a groundbreaking power that shapes points of view, encourages decisive reasoning, and adds to the more extensive human story. The unconditional investigation of information turns into a wellspring of strengthening, freedom, and a developing appreciation for the tremendousness of the scholarly scene.

In the expert domain, the unassuming prospects become an impetus for development, imagination, and the quest for significant commitments. The hero perceives that a vocation is definitely not a decent direction however a unique way with space for rehash, investigation, and the arrangement of individual qualities with proficient pursuits. The end drawn is that the unconditional idea of the expert excursion takes into consideration flexibility, versatility, and the development of a feeling of direction that rises above the limits of a traditional profession way.

The hero approaches proficient undertakings with a receptiveness to unanticipated open doors, challenges, and the potential for development in surprising headings. The unconditional potential outcomes in the expert circle become a wellspring of strengthening, empowering the hero to embrace change, explore vulnerabilities, and diagram a course that lines up with individual yearnings and cultural commitments.

Cultural commitment takes on another aspect as the hero explores the unconditional opportunities for adding to aggregate prosperity. The acknowledgment that cultural stories are liquid, dependent on future developments, and molded by individual activities encourages a feeling of obligation and a pledge to good effect. The hero turns into a cognizant member in the continuous development of cultural standards, values, and yearnings.

The unassuming investigation of cultural commitments includes a readiness to challenge standards, advocate for equity, and take part in the cooperative work to make positive change. The end drawn is that the hero, as an individual from the cultural embroidery, has the organization to impact the course of aggregate stories, adding to a more comprehensive, humane, and reasonable future.

Inwardly, the unassuming prospects become a wellspring of versatility and a more profound comprehension of the human experience. The hero explores the back and forth movement of feelings with a feeling of receptiveness to weakness, recognizing that profound extravagance lies in the eagerness to profoundly feel. The end drawn is that personal investigation includes the highs of delight as well as the profundities of distress, and both add to the nuanced and significant embroidery of life.

The unconditional opportunities for future experiences and investigations stretch out past the natural scenes of the known. The hero embraces the call of the neglected, whether it be in actual travel, scholarly pursuits, or the domains of innovativeness and creative mind. The end is that the excursion is an encouragement to step past safe places, to embrace vulnerability, and to delight in the thrill of the strange.

Travel, as a similitude for the unconditional investigation of the world, turns into an extraordinary encounter for the hero. The acknowledgment that the world is an immense embroidery of societies, scenes, and stories urges the hero to leave on ventures that rise above the limits of commonality. The unconditional potential outcomes in movement become a wellspring of social improvement, growing points of view, and cultivating a worldwide mindfulness that rises above borders.

Innovativeness and creative articulation become roads for the unassuming investigation of the creative mind. The hero perceives that the domains of workmanship, writing, and imaginative undertakings are boundless in their true capacity for self-articulation and revelation. The end drawn is that inventiveness isn't restricted to a particular medium however is a limitless power that considers the investigation of feelings, thoughts, and the boundless potential outcomes of the human creative mind.

The normal world, with its stunning magnificence and intricacy, turns into a material for the unassuming investigation of natural cognizance. The hero draws in with nature not just as a detached onlooker but rather as a steward of the planet, perceiving the interconnectedness between human prosperity and the soundness of the Earth. The unassuming prospects in natural investigation become a source of inspiration, moving the hero to add to reasonable practices, preservation endeavors, and a feeling of obligation toward people in the future.

In the calm snapshots of consideration, the hero thinks about the unconditional conceivable outcomes that stretch across the immense embroidery of the steadily unfurling venture. The determination is definitely not a decent endpoint yet an acknowledgment that the excursion is a continuous discourse with the obscure — a hug of the secrets that anticipate, the difficulties that shape, and the delights that enlighten the way forward.

The unassuming prospects become a way of thinking of living — a way to deal with the excursion that is portrayed by a feeling of transparency, interest, and an eagerness to embrace the vulnerabilities that accompany the unexplored world. The hero remains at the convergence of past and future, mixed with the mindfulness that each step in the right direction is an investigation, each decision is an experience, and each second is a chance for new disclosures.

As the hero pushes ahead, impelled by the force of unconditional conceivable outcomes, there is a feeling of freedom — an affirmation that the excursion isn't bound to the pages previously composed however is a story that keeps on unfurling with endless potential.

The determination, subsequently, isn't a goodbye however a preface to the following part — a confirmation that the steadily unfurling venture is a timeless hit the dance floor with the boundless potential outcomes that anticipate in the endless field representing things to come.

As the hero remains at the edge representing things to come, the skyline unfurls with the commitment of unknown domains, alluring toward future experiences and investigations. The acknowledgment sunrises that the excursion is a powerful story, constantly developing, and the material of potential outcomes extends limitlessly before them.

In the domain of self-disclosure, the hero considers the future to be a sweeping scene of likely development and contemplation. The excursion inside, an interminable investigation of personality, values, and yearnings, stretches out into the distance of the unexplored world. The comprehension that oneself is certainly not a decent element however an embroidery woven with the strings of involvement and mindfulness pushes the hero toward the unconditional conceivable outcomes of individual development.

What's to come turns into a chance for the hero to dive further into the layers of their being, to stand up to difficulties with versatility, and to embrace the unfurling story of self-revelation. It is an acknowledgment that the excursion inside is a long lasting campaign, rich with the possibility of revealing secret features of oneself and exploring the steadily changing scene of self-awareness.

In the immense breadth of connections, what's to come is imagined as a mosaic of associations ready to be shaped and supported. The hero perceives that the excursion of connections isn't restricted to the past however stretches out into the unlimited domains representing things to come. Kinships, familial bonds, and heartfelt associations are viewed as strings that wind through the embroidery of life, with unconditional opportunities for new experiences and extended associations.

The hero moves toward the future with a feeling of receptiveness to different connections, recognizing that every collaboration holds the potential for common development and shared encounters. The comprehension that connections are not static however powerful, developing elements urges the hero to embrace the vulnerabilities representing things to come, encouraging associations that rise above the limits of commonality and social contrasts.

Chasing after information, what's to come unfurls as a neglected landscape of scholarly interest and disclosure. The hero imagines an excursion of ceaseless learning, with the acknowledgment that the quest for information has no limits. The unassuming prospects in scholarly investigation become a wellspring of motivation, driving the hero to address suppositions, challenge predispositions, and adventure into unfamiliar domains of understanding.

Whether through proper instruction, free review, or drawing in with different disciplines, the hero sees the future as a scene where the skylines of information grow perpetually. The delight of revelation, the excitement of uncovering new viewpoints, and the fulfillment of adding to the aggregate storehouse of human grasping become directing stars in the heavenly body of future scholarly undertakings.

The expert excursion, saw from the perspective representing things to come, turns into a story of development, versatility, and significant commitments. The hero perceives that the vocation way is definitely not a direct direction yet a powerful scene with open doors for rehash and investigation. Unassuming conceivable outcomes in the expert domain convert into a mentality of versatility, flexibility, and a promise to reason driven tries.

What's in store is imagined as a material for imaginative articulation and creative commitments to the expert circle. The hero embraces that each profession decision, each venture embraced, and every joint effort went into is a stage toward forming a story that lines up with individual qualities and goals. The comprehension that the expert excursion is a continuum of learning and development urges the hero to move toward the future with a feeling of direction and a feeling of advancement.

In the cultural story, what's to come is viewed as a field for positive effect and significant commitment. The hero perceives the interconnectedness between private activities and the more extensive cultural setting, seeing the future as a chance to add to positive change. Unconditional potential outcomes in cultural contribution become a call to advocate for equity, balance, and maintainability, encouraging a feeling of obligation toward the aggregate prosperity.

What's in store is imagined as an opportunity to effectively take part in forming cultural standards, values, and desires. The hero sees open doors for local area commitment, joint effort with similar people and associations, and a pledge to leaving a positive engraving on the cultural embroidery. The comprehension that each individual has the organization to add to the aggregate story urges the hero to move toward the future with a feeling of office and a devotion to making an additional comprehensive and humane world.

Inwardly, what's to come is viewed as a material for the statement of a rich and nuanced scope of sentiments. The hero recognizes that close to home investigation is a continuous excursion, with unassuming opportunities for encountering bliss, distress, love, and versatility. What's in store turns into a space for developing capacity to understand people on a profound level, exploring intricacies, and encouraging a profound association with oneself as well as other people.

The hero moves toward the future with a receptiveness to weakness, understanding that profound wealth lies in the readiness to feel and communicate a range of feelings truly. The unconditional potential outcomes in profound investigation become a wellspring of solidarity, permitting the hero to explore the steadily changing scene of individual sentiments and relational elements with a feeling of genuineness and strength.

In the domain of movement and actual investigation, what's in store unfurls as a guide of undertakings ready to be left upon. The hero imagines excursions to new scenes, social encounters, and regular miracles, perceiving that the world is a huge embroidery of variety and magnificence. The unconditional potential outcomes in movement become a wellspring of motivation, empowering the hero to step past natural limits and embrace the excitement of the unexplored world.

What's in store is viewed as an opportunity to drench oneself in various societies, to interface with individuals from different foundations, and to observe the miracles of the world. The hero embraces that movement isn't simply an actual development yet an extraordinary encounter that widens points of view, cultivates social comprehension, and adds to self-awareness.

Inventiveness and creative articulation are seen as boundless domains of future investigation. The hero perceives that what's to come is an open material for innovative undertakings, whether through visual expressions, writing, music, or any type of imaginative articulation. The unconditional potential outcomes in imagination become a wellspring of opportunity, permitting the hero to try, enhance, and add to the steadily developing embroidery of human creative articulation.

What's in store is imagined as an opportunity to push the limits of imaginative investigation, to embrace the obscure chasing original thoughts and creative tasks. The hero moves toward the future with a feeling of fun loving nature, understanding that imagination flourishes in a climate of interest, trial and error, and the readiness to face creative challenges.

Natural cognizance turns into a point of convergence later on, with the hero seeing unassuming opportunities for maintainable living and biological stewardship. The acknowledgment that the prosperity of the planet is unpredictably associated with individual activities urges the hero to imagine an eventual fate of capable and careful ecological practices. The unassuming prospects in ecological investigation become a source of inspiration, motivating the hero to add to preservation endeavors, advocate for maintainable practices, and develop a feeling of obligation toward the Earth.

In the tranquil snapshots of examination, the hero thinks about the tremendous scene of unassuming conceivable outcomes that what's to come holds. The end drawn isn't one of certainty however of expectation — an acknowledgment that the excursion is a continuous discourse with potential, a persistent investigation of the consistently unfurling story of life.

The unassuming opportunities for future experiences and investigations become a way of thinking of living — a way to deal with the excursion described by a feeling of transparency, interest, and an eagerness to embrace the vulnerabilities that accompany the unexplored world. The hero stands ready at the edge representing things to come, injected with the mindfulness that each step in the right direction is an investigation, each decision is an experience, and each second is a chance for new revelations.

As the hero pushes ahead, moved by the energy of unassuming conceivable outcomes, there is a feeling of freedom — an affirmation that the excursion isn't bound to the pages previously composed however is a story that keeps on unfurling with limitless potential. The decision, thusly, isn't a goodbye yet a preface to the following section — a confirmation that the consistently unfurling venture is an everlasting hit the dance floor with the boundless potential outcomes that anticipate in the endless scope representing things to come.

www.ingramcontent.com/pod-product-compliance
Lightning Source LLC
LaVergne TN
LVHW011945070526
838202LV00054B/4799